CAREER PLANNING FOR HIGH-SCHOOL STUDENTS

THE CAREER MANAGEMENT ESSENTIALS (CME)

ADRIAN GONZALEZ

ISBN: 978-1-64516-505-7   (Paperback Edition)
ISBN: 978-1-64516-504-0   (Hardcover Edition)
ISBN: 978-1-64516-506-4   (E-book Edition)

Some characters and events in this book are fictitious. Any similarity to real persons, living or dead, is coincidental and not intended by the author.

Book Ordering Information

Phone Number: 347-901-4929 or 347-901-4920
Email: info@globalsummithouse.com
Global Summit House
www.globalsummithouse.com

Printed in the United States of America

CONTENTS

WHO IS CME FOR?

To find out, answer yes or no to the following questions:

Are you a high school student? _____

Are you undecided about your future career? _____

Are you the parent or guardian of a high school student? _____

Do you have a friend or a family member currently in middle school or high school? _____

Are you a high school teacher or administrator? _____

Are you a career coach? _____

Are you a high school counselor? _____

Are you the parent of a middle school student? _____

Are you a student counselor working for a post-secondary school? _____

Are you a public figure interested in the subject of education? _____

If your answer is yes to at least of one of these questions, you need CME.

WHAT IS CME AND WHAT IS GOING TO DO FOR YOU?

CME stands for *Career Management Essentials*; it is a concept that is explained by combining the definition of each of its words:

Career: a profession that someone does for a long time (e.g., 50 to 60 years).

Management: the act of controlling and making decisions.

Essential: the very basic thing you need to know.

Put these three meanings together and CME is defined as the *basic knowledge you need to control what you are going to be doing professionally for next 50 to 60 years*. Say "CME" aloud and fast and you will hear yourself saying… See me! Like if you were predicting how you would see yourself professionally five years from now.

The key word in CME is *management* because it establishes that you are the manager of your own career; the one **in charge**, who causes your professional future to take one direction or another. The next word is *essential*; this is to emphasize that the basic thing you need to know as your own career manager is to foresee problems and take corrective actions before they happen. In career managing, there are **three problems** that you need to plan and anticipate for. They are 1) high unemployment, 2) low college degree utilization, and 3) student loan defaulting. *CME is the solution for all three of them.*

High unemployment rate among recent graduates: You need to be aware that when you graduate, whether from college, high school, or a vocational school, you may not be able to find a job. According to the US Bureau of Labor Statistics, in July of 2014, the unemployment rate reached **11.4** (for workers ages 20-24) and **20** (for workers ages 16-19). Now, compare these two rates against same month and year total unemployment rate of **6.2**.

Low college degree utilization: You also need to be aware that you may have worked hard to earn that college degree, spent an average of **$50,000** to **$100,000,** and still not get to use it or get properly compensated for it. A survey conducted by CareerBuilder revealed that about **47%** of college graduates claimed <u>not</u> to have started in the workforce through jobs that were related to their major. In fact, **32%** never got to work in jobs related to their major at all. But what is scary is that **62%** of these same graduates are working in jobs that don't even require a college degree.[1]

Student loan defaulting: In September of 2014, the national student loan default rate stood as high as 13.7%. According to an article by the Washington Post,[2] the government was said to have sanctioned at least 21 post-secondary schools for incurring student's loan default rates of as high as **30%** for three consecutive years or **40%** within a year (Nick, 2014).

CME is a strategy specifically designed to address these three problems. When students graduate from high school, they move from a "leading by the hand" system to a new "you are on your own" reality. This drastic change is caused by the distinctive objectives among these two educational levels. The objective of the elementary and secondary education is to provide the academic foundation the student needs to succeed at a post-secondary academic level, but the objective of the post-secondary education is to train the student in whatever **specific skills** he or she chooses. For example, a male student enrolled in a university to study Anthropology the will be taught how to study primates in Africa. Upon graduation, this same student cannot go back to the university to complain that nobody told him that there were no jobs in this field so now he has no money to pay the debt. Why would the school be held responsible? They did what the student paid them to do. He left the school being an expert in African primates. In this same manner, it is not the school's fault that when you finished a Bachelor in Business Administration degree you had to start with a minimum-wage job because you had no previous **work experience.** According to them (the post-secondary school), you should have figured that out on your own.

The reality is that when students are left on their own, they fail repeatedly at **establishing connections with employers** while they are still in school. They don't bother to do so until they are heavily in debt and desperately looking for a job after graduation. When students choose careers with no guidance or supervision, these decisions are based, most of the time, on mentally fabricated dream jobs. After graduation, the students must go out into the real world to see for themselves if these dream jobs exist, like our friend the Anthropologist. By the time reality hits, they are thousands of dollars in debt, and the most productive years of life (no wife, no husband, and no kids) are already gone. CME wants you to be prepared by making informed decisions with a realistic objective in mind and not be surprised like most graduates.

The statistics presented above are the proof that *today's job market shows <u>no mercy</u> with those students who <u>do not</u> begin early to shape their education to fulfill employers' needs.*

The saddest part of all this is that it could have been avoided if students would have simply asked the **right questions of the right people.** Stop here for a moment and look at the CME flow chart on the next page. We want you to see with your own eyes what we really mean by *asking the right questions to the right people.* Notice how each step poses a question. These questions are designed to gain information about employers' specific requirements so that high school class selection, majors, and extracurricular activities can be directed at meeting those qualifications. Then, see also how each step identifies a **subject matter expert.** These are the professionals with the training and experience; to guide the student through the actions he or she needs to take to answer the question presented in the step. In the chapters ahead, or should we say in the next four years of your life, you will see how CME creates a collaboration platform where multiple areas of expertise come together for the first time for a common goal. CME *streamlines* the guidance of economists, career coaches, human resource managers, school counselors, and teachers to ensure that when you graduate you have already performed the tasks employers need and you have been trained in the specific skills they are looking for. Put another way, CME teaches how to capture the type of knowledge and work experience employers are looking for, and then translate it into things you can do, while still in school, to show them that you already know and can do the job, even though you just graduated. This kind of <u>early connection</u> with employers is what leads to employment, degree utilization, and financial independence at any level of educational attainment. It determines your ability to compete, not only in the job market, but also for admission into prestigious colleges, universities, and vocational schools after high school. The final goal of this book is that when you graduate, your resume matches your chosen job qualifications in terms of education and work experience.

CME JOB AID

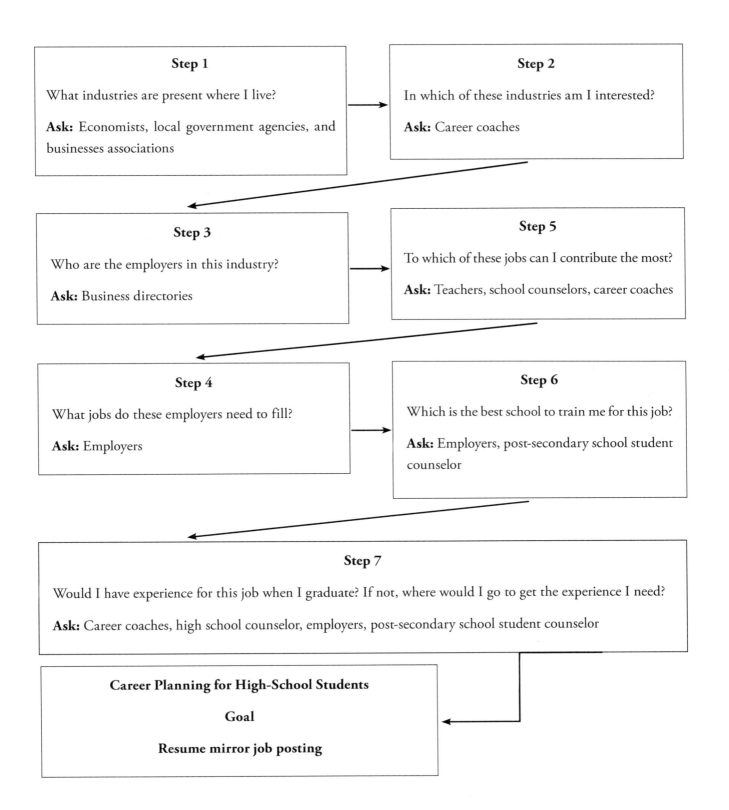

Step 1

What industries are present where I live?

Ask: Economists, local government agencies, and businesses associations

Step 2

In which of these industries am I interested?

Ask: Career coaches

Step 3

Who are the employers in this industry?

Ask: Business directories

Step 5

To which of these jobs can I contribute the most?

Ask: Teachers, school counselors, career coaches

Step 4

What jobs do these employers need to fill?

Ask: Employers

Step 6

Which is the best school to train me for this job?

Ask: Employers, post-secondary school student counselor

Step 7

Would I have experience for this job when I graduate? If not, where would I go to get the experience I need?

Ask: Career coaches, high school counselor, employers, post-secondary school student counselor

Career Planning for High-School Students

Goal

Resume mirror job posting

CME KEY POINTS

The key points to remember are:

- CME is a strategy designed to capture employers' job requirements and translate them into specific actions you can take while in school to meet those requirements (e.g., selection of classes and extracurricular activities, etc.)
- The strategy is broken down in baby steps. Each step presents a task (in the form of a question), then it identifies the helper(s) that will provide the assistance needed to complete the task (answer the question).
- The outcome of each step's task (or answer) is captured in a Career Worksheet. This form becomes your career plan.
- When the last step is reached, your resume at the time of graduation from a post-secondary school matches (or mirrors) the qualifications of a chosen job position (education and work experience) even though you just finished school.

Once your reading of the entire book is completed, you are going to hand it over to your parents for them to do the same. The next section titled Message for Parents is directed at them. CME also provides guidance for your parents on how to facilitate and ov ersee the career decision process every step of the way. When your parents finish with the book, both of you together are going to go to the CME checklist. This is the starting point. All CME tasks are organized into a comprehensive checklist that covers from 9th grade to the 12th grade to allow you and your parents to track progress toward the CME goal.

MESSAGE FOR PARENTS

A major part of CME success is parents' involvement. CME encourages you to work with your son or daughter as a team, and to follow the guidance provided in this book for every step. It is your duty as a parent to do so. A supportive environment is created by actively educating yourself on how to carry out this responsibility. CME provides specific guidance for parents on how to facilitate the task required for each step, as well as on how to support the interactions with the different helpers. CME expects you to be present during the entire process; you are your children's advocate, personal career coach, and career facilitator. In this section, we are going to limit ourselves to explaining why you need to get involved, and give you your first assignment.

As the parent of a high school student, you need to be aware that failure to become an overseer your child's career decision may affect your own **financial** situation in the very near future. Taking no action may result in you having to support children financially after graduation from collage. Having to support your children financially (when you were not supposed to) can prevent you from allocating additional budget for retirement and/or to care for your elderly parents. Our hearts go out to the millions of American parents who have withdrawn money from their retirement funds to cover their children's education thinking that a college degree would guarantee them a job and a better future (this is no longer a guarantee). Children are young and have plenty of time to pay back student's loans, but you, because of your age and the stock market performance, might not be able to recover it by the time you need it the most.

Having said this, here is your first CME assignment: Discuss with your son or daughter the "the school as my employer" attitude.

As a parent or guardian, it is critical that you always support your child's teacher, especially when it comes to discipline (unless it involves an illegal or an unethical situation). It is your duty to teach your children to respect and to be subject to authority (this is only learned at home). Later in the workforce, teachers will be replaced by employers; therefore, you need to be aware (and make your child aware as well) that in the absence of work experience, good grades and academic achievements are the ONLY references that employers can rely on to determine if your child is a hardworking, dedicated, and disciplined job candidate. Grades and academic recognitions are FACTS that show your child's level of performance in tasks assigned to him or her. They are the equivalent of a job review. Job recruiters are advising their clients to list on their resumes their grades (only if they are competitive) together with accomplishments and recognition from their teachers that will make them stand out from the crowd. According to them, employers look for hardworking individuals whose school's performance proves that they can bring a benefit or something of value to their organization (e.g., increase production or bring improvements to a product/ service they provide).

For many students, the damage is already done when they realized how important this was. Therefore, CME encourages you to teach your children to approach their schoolwork and teachers as if they were already working for an actual employer. The school context is very like the context provided by any job setting. You have a boss that tells you what tasks need to be done (the teacher); you have expectations for academic performance; there are norms of behavior (e.g., projects/assignments with specific objectives, guidelines, and deadlines).

Due to these similarities, the school setting can provide the context for concrete evidence of hard work and dedication, which eventually will lead to early career accomplishments, recognition, and recommendations from your teachers. These early career accomplishments are what later become visible to employers and prestigious post-secondary schools, affecting their decision to either hire or accept your children into their programs.

There is a direct correlation between employment after graduation and a person's level of performance. Therefore, by establishing this attitude at home, we are hopeful that the student takes advantage of the different opportunities to excel that the school setting provides; opportunities such as project-based learning. This new trend in education gives children an opportunity to demonstrate their critical thinking and problem-solving skills. School administrators finally woke up to the reality that the reason people have jobs is to solve problems. Consequently, soon (if not happening already), students are going to be required to show their thought process for every answer they give in class, either by explaining how they arrived at that conclusion or by drawing a diagram of the critical thinking process that produced their response). When you reinforce in your children the "school as my employer" mind-set at an early age, they are likely to have <u>fewer</u> work/performance issues later in life when school is replaced by an employer (e.g., following instructions, respect for authority). And this is ultimately what CME is trying to accomplish here.

CHAPTER 1
WHAT INDUSTRIES ARE PRESENT WHERE I LIVE? (STEP 1)

Imagine for a second that you are a tailor whose job is to design a suit that would perfectly fit a client. To do this right, the first thing to do is find out who will be wearing the suit, then take his or her measurements. After this is done, the cutting and sewing begin. In this illustration, the client is your future employer and the tailoring process represents the actual career planning process broken down in steps. When the last step is reached, your resume will fit the employer's job opening, just like a suit specially designed to fit a tailor's client. Just like the tailor in this illustration, if you want to start training and gaining experience for the specific skills employers are looking for, while in school, you need to first know who your employers are so their measurement can be taken, figuratively speaking.

The two key words in Step 1's question are *industries* and *present*. Why do you think this is? Well, because by knowing the industries or professional fields that are present where you live, that is how you find out who your future employers are. Here is another illustration: Let's say that you give a surprise visit to a friend you haven't seen for a while. This friend is a passionate baseball fan and a board member of the community's baseball club. If this were the case, where would you go to find him? It is not hard to figure out the answer. You would probably seek him at the club's next board meeting. Just like in this illustration, employers can be found in the different social clubs they belong to.

Most employers belong to an industry sector or a national professional association that identifies them and sets the rules of their game, figuratively speaking. CME refers to an industry or professional field as the classification (or separation) of businesses according to the type of service or product they provide to the people. For example, a business that sells cars is in a separate category than a business that does banking or provides health care. Going back to this illustration, you can say that all car dealers belong to one social club and all financial or health care institutions belong to another social club. What CME is trying to show you here is that for you to find out who your employers are, you need to list the industry sectors that operate in your area where you live. This local employer's social club hunting is called *industry research*. There are two main reasons to conduct industry research:

1. Career decisions are made at the industry level and not at the occupational level.

2. Industry research gives focus and direction to career exploration.

Having a career does not mean that you picked an occupation in which you will be working for the rest of your life. Instead, it means that you chose an industry or professional field of which to take part. A search in the dictionary reveals the following definitions:

Career: A *profession pursued as a permanent calling; a course of continued progress or activity.*
Occupation: *Duties/tasks; a job position at which one regularly works for pay.*

You choose a career when you decide the type of <u>service</u> or <u>product</u> you want to contribute to society (permanent calling… continued progress). That is choice of what type of industry to be part of, and <u>not</u> choosing an occupation. Occupations are job positions within the industry. Here are some examples:

Careers (A chosen Industry)	Occupations (What you do within the industry, your role or function)
Health Care Industry	Nurse, nurse assistant, physician, health administrator, X-ray technician, physical therapist, etc.
Finance Industry	Teller, loan officer, relation banker, financial advisor, insurance agent, etc.
Education Industry	Elementary teacher, school principal, college associate professor, school administrator, etc.

Once a career or industry is decided on, it <u>should not be changed</u> (*a professional field pursued as a <u>permanent calling and course of continued progress</u>*), while occupations, on the other hand, are always changing. Occupations are defined by the actual tasks performed on the job and <u>employers are the ones who decide what tasks need to get done to fulfill their customers' demand.</u> As a result, some job positions/occupations disappear and others emerge. Occupations are always evolving.

Here are some examples of what is considered a career change and what is not. If your high school math teacher become the school's assistance principal or the head of the Math Department and no longer teaches in the classroom, this change is <u>not</u> considered a career change, for he or she is still in the education industry, though job tasks have changed (occupation). However, if he or she goes to work as a loan officer at your local bank, then that is considered a career change, for he or she has moved from the education industry to the finance industry.

Here it is another example. A nurse assistant decides to go back to school to become a registered nurse or a physician. This, also, is <u>not</u> considered a career change, for he or she remains in the same industry, although his or her occupation has changed.

Now let's say that later in life you realized you made the wrong decision and want to change careers (as in changing industries). Is it possible? Absolutely. Do we recommend it? Definitely not. When you do this, it is possible that you are going to have a hard time finding a job. First, you are going to be competing against people already in the industry, with years of experience and knowledge that you don't have. And second, financially it could be a major setback because responsibilities increase with age (child support, marriage, mortgage payment, etc.) and they become an obstacle hard to overcome if further education is required. Although people change careers all the time and some are successful, this is not a wise attitude at this life stage.

With this distinction in mind, let's discuss how industry research directs career exploration. As strange as this might seem, we would like to ask you a non-related question: Does a goldfish grow as large as its enclosure? The answer is yes. When a goldfish is kept in a small tank it is poisoned by its own waste. Its growth gets stunted and it eventually dies. However, when you give a goldfish plenty of room to swim, provide good filtration, and perform the recommended water changes, you can have a full-grown goldfish that can live over 25 years. Likewise, the industry in which you choose to launch a career is like the size of the tank to the goldfish.

CME Job Aid sets parameters on career exploration in a way that leads you to choose industries where there is plenty of room to thrive and where your career growth/opportunities will not get stunted for they are founded on consumer demand. Consumer demand is what people want and want to pay for, and it refers to a service or product. It is also considered the fuel that keeps your career going forward, just like gasoline in a car. You find consumer demand by simply taking a closer look at the businesses around your area. Businesses are strategically located as a response to consumer demand and the unique characteristics of the area that makes it favorable for the type of industry (e.g., natural resources, export-import infrastructure [basic physical and organizational structures and facilities, such as buildings, roads, and power supplies needed for the operation of an enterprise], and demographics [statistical data relating to the population and particular groups within it], as well as other factors specific to industries). When you do an industry research of your local economy, you are taking advantage of the fact that the experts in consumer demand and commercial developers already did 50 percent of your career planning legwork for you. Through their behind-the-scenes findings, these business experts are showing you the industries/careers that you need to focus on. When career exploration is not set within the limits of industry presence, career planning is like finding a needle in a haystack, and the trick to finding that needle is to reduce the size of the haystack. There are thousands of possible occupations, some of them constantly appearing and disappearing, but there are a little over a hundred almost unchanging industries. This much smaller number is further reduced as you discover that not all these industries are present where you live.

DEFINING THE AREA WHERE YOU LIVE

The number one reason for unemployment after graduation is failure to connect with an employer while still in school. Therefore, the CME Job Aid leads you to establish contact with employers in your community as early as 9th grade. To do this you must be able to show up on time for any interaction. Draw a radius of one-hour maximum of commuting time from where you live; this will define your area. But, what happens if you move after graduation? If you move after graduation you have nothing to lose. If the same industries are present where you move to, then there is no harm done. But if there are different industries, then there are always skills that can transfer from one industry to others (e.g., customer service skills, office technology, report writing skills, oral communication, etc.). Also, early career accomplishments such as letters, commendations, and employer's recognition follow you wherever you go. In any situation, you will be better off than having no experience at all. However, if you live in a rural area, you should include the nearest major city in your industry research.

STEP 1 HELPERS - ECONOMISTS

To answer Step 1's question you are going to need the assistance of economists and local government agencies. Economists study the production and distribution of goods and services. They collect and analyze data, research trends, and evaluate economic issues. Like doctors, they take an X-ray of your area and tell you where job opportunities are (strong industry sectors with a positive outlook) and where there could be trouble (weakening industries). To answer Step 1's question you have to list the industries operating in your area (one-hour maximum of commuting time to include a nearby major city). If you live close to a county or city line you may have to access more than one local government agency. You can access economists' reports and commentaries for free by visiting your county or city's official website. Once on the website, look for headers or links with titles such as: Economic Development, Labor Market Report, Analysis of Current Economic Trends, Economic & Demographics Profiles, etc. Also, it is important to incorporate your findings into your high school course selection as soon as possible. For example, an economic note on Miami-Dade County (South Florida) states that Miami's economy is based on tourism and export/import, being considered the bridge between the continental United States and the rest of the Americas. Based just on this piece of information, wouldn't you think that to be employable in Miami you are going to need Spanish and Portuguese as a second language and that perhaps this is something you can learn while in school? Even if you move out of Miami, don't you get a "choose option #2 for Spanish" every time you dial a 1-800 number? This is one of the many examples of things you can find during industry research on which you can act to make yourself employable, while still in high school.

INDUSTRY RESEARCH ACTIVITY

Instructions: Visit http://www.bls.gov/iag/tgs/iag_index_alpha.htm for a complete list of industries, with their corresponding NAIC code. Then, using the local resources, eliminate from the list the industries that are <u>NOT</u> present where you live. **NAICS** stands for the North American Industry Classification System, a standard system used by the government to classify business institutions according the services they provide. *At the end of this activity you should be able to come up with a list of the industries that are present in the area where you live.* Look at the sample provided to see how it is supposed to look to include notes and reminders you can write for yourself.

Employment area: Miami-Dade County (South Florida)

Websites/ Resources:

http://www.miamidade.gov/business/economic-development.asp
http://www.beaconcouncil.com/

Industries Found

Air Transportation (NAICS 481)

- Repair and Maintenance
- Air operations

Trade and Logistics

Retail Trade (NAICS 44-45)

- Motor Vehicle and Parts Dealers (NAICS 441)
- Furniture and Home Furnishings Stores (NAICS 442)
- Electronics and Appliance Stores (NAICS 443)
- Building Material and Garden Equipment and Supplies Dealers (NAICS 444)
- Food and Beverage Stores (NAICS 445)
- Health and Personal Care Stores (NAICS 446)
- Gasoline Stations (NAICS 447)
- Clothing and Clothing Accessories Stores (NAICS 448)
- General Merchandise Stores (NAICS 452)
- Miscellaneous Store Retailers (NAICS 453)
- Non-store Retailers (NAICS 454)
- Merchant Wholesalers Durable goods (cars, furniture, industrial equipment, etc.) (NAICS 423)

- Merchant Wholesalers Non-durable goods (paper products, chemical products, drugs, textile products, apparel, footwear, etc.) (NAICS 424)

Logistics

- Warehousing and Storage (NAICS 493)
- Wholesale Electronic Markets and Agents and Brokers (NAICS 425)
- Wholesale Trade (NAICS 42)
- Truck Transportation (NAICS 484)

Note: Every region of the world is present in Miami's international trade and logistics network. There are about 300 freight forwarders and customs brokers companies.

Health Care Services

- Ambulatory Health Services (NAICS 621)
- Health Care and Social Assistance (NAICS 452)
- Hospitals (NAICS 622)
- Nursing and Residential Care Facilities (NAICS 623)

Note: Miami is home to leaders in the health care industry such as Beckman Coulter, BD Biosciences, Cordis (a Johnson & Johnson Company) and Merck.

Hospitality and Leisure

- Accommodation and Food Services (NAICS 72)
- Food Services and Drinking Places (NAICS 722)

Note: Miami is considered one of the top urban resorts in the world and a favored location for business meetings, sales events, and trade shows, including high-profile political and religious events.

Banking and Finance

- Finance and Insurance (NAICS 52)
- Funds, Trusts, and other financial vehicles (NAICS 525)

Note: Miami has the largest concentration of domestic and international banks on the East Coast after New York City. It includes private banking and wealth management and trade finance.

Professional Services

- Legal Services (NAICS 5411)
- Accounting, Tax Preparation, Bookkeeping, and Payroll Services (NAICS 5412)
- Architectural, Engineering, and Related Services (NAICS 5413)
- Specialized Design Services (NAICS 5414)
- Computer Systems Design and Related Services (NAICS 5415)
- Management, Scientific, and Technical Consulting Services (NAICS 5416)
- Advertising and Related Services (NAICS 5418)
- Real Estate and Rental and Leasing (NAICS 53)
- Administrative and Support Services (NAICS 561)
- Repair and Maintenance (NAICS 811)
  - Automotive Repair and Maintenance (NAICS 8111)
  - Electronic and Precision Equipment Repair and Maintenance (NAICS 8112)
  - Commercial and Industrial Machinery and Equipment (except Automotive and Electronic) Repair and Maintenance (NAICS 8113)

With simple online research, you and your parents are going to be able to considerably reduce the size of the career haystack. Even though you don't know yet who they are (so the measurement can be taken and the tailoring can begin), you are just one step further in knowing where to find them (what social club they are going to belong to). In the sample provided, this Miami student was able to bring down his career options to about 46 possible industries, including subsectors. This number of possible careers can be further reduced; in Step 2, coming up next, you will learn how this is done.

STEP 1 GUIDANCE FOR PARENTS

Step 1's objective can be summarized in three words: industry, industry, and industry. If you ask a realtor what are the three most important things to remember in the real estate business, he or she would say: location, location, location. This common phrase reminds homeowners that the determining factors in the value of their house is the location. A house can be remodeled, demolished, and/or rebuilt, but can't change its location. How desirable the location of the property is determines how fast the house is going to be sold and how high the price is going to be. In this illustration, location represents the industry in which your son or daughter chooses to build his or her career; the house refers to an occupation (always being upgraded) and value is how fast he or she is going to get hired after graduation (how desirable the skills are he or she is going to train for). With this in mind, you can say that the objective of Step 1 was to teach your child how to find a good location (industry) to build their career. Therefore, CME is going to ask that you assist your child in the search and interpretation of economic data so he or she can come up with their own list of possible careers as accurately as possible.

– NOTES –

CHAPTER 2
WHICH OF THESE INDUSTRIES AM I INTERESTED IN? (STEP 2)

The key word in this question is *interested*. Interest is defined as:

1. The state of wanting to know about something.

2. The quality of making someone curious or holding their attention.

Consider this following illustration. Imagine for a second that you had to take a class continuously for the rest of your life. Wouldn't you want to make sure to pick a subject that would make you curious and want to know more? These classes do exist; grownups call it continuing education. Continuing education means you will be bound to study the same subject until your mid-seventies (possible retirement age, according to the social security office projections). Picture this for a second; at eight o'clock in the morning, as soon as you report to work, you will read hundreds of e-mails about this same subject, then, the phone will ring, and people will start asking you questions and talking about their problems with, you guessed…. the same subject. Choosing an industry based on interest is how you ensure that you are going to stay motivated and focused in school and at work. Interest influences your academic and work performance, and both employers and post-secondary schools will consider your performance and accomplishments to choose one candidate over another. The bottom line is that interest should be your motivation to enter into a particular industry; however, you won't know if something is interesting until you test it out.

Talking about testing things out, in the following illustration you can see how testing a career is a very similar process to buying a new car. The first step of car buying is to determine your budget (how much you can afford). Once you figure out that number, you are going to make a list of cars available within the boundaries of your budget. In Step 1, you did something similar, when you came up with a list of possible careers within the limits or boundaries of consumer demand, namely, industry presence. Second, the car buyer researches online each of these models to see which of them catches their **interest** (e.g., looks at photos and reads tons of information about the car). Did you know that 80 percent of car buyers research different cars online for several months before they decide to walk in to a car dealer? In this same way, you are going to research each of these industries online before you go to the actual field to contact an employee in the industry or embark on what CME calls a "career test drive."

As you go through the Industry of Interest Activity coming up next, use interest to progressively eliminate industries from the list you created in Step 1. Interest can be uncovered by asking questions like the ones found below:

- What kind of problems do you like to solve? For example, neighbors are always coming to you so you can fix their computer.
- What kind of questions do people come to you for help with? For what services or products? For example, friends call you all the time to ask you what software program they should buy for their computer.
- What is the most typical topic that would get started in a conversation? For example, the latest informational technology news.
- When you are in the magazine section of a library/bookstore, what type of magazine do you usually pick up? For example: *PCWorld*, *Technews*, or any other technology publication.
- As you go through the "finding your interest" activities, ask yourself what experience did you enjoy the most? And what made it so? For example, going to a technology trade show and watching demonstrations of the latest technology.
- What academic subjects do you prefer in school? For example: computer science.

INDUSTRY OF INTEREST ACTIVITY

Imagine if you were test driving careers at the occupational level, how long would that take? Some online occupational databases boast of having about 20,000-plus occupations. Before you and you parents get on the road, wasting time and gasoline, there are some industries that can be eliminated from the comfort of your home or nearby library. Here are some recommendations:

1. Research online for information about each of the industries listed in Step 1. Look at the product and/or service they provide to the people. You can start by simply typing the name of the industry in the search box of any search engine (e.g., Google, Yahoo, YouTube, etc.). There is no fixed amount of time to spend on each industry. Some of them you will know right away, and some others might take you a little longer. Always give yourself plenty time with each industry and consult various sources. As you are doing this research, ask yourself, do I want to read more about this? If the answer is no, cross out that industry from your list. But if the answer is yes, proceed to item 2.

2. In your local library, look for industry magazines and journals. In these publications, you not only can read about hot topics and pressing issues in the industry, but also find articles about leading professionals in the field and company profiles (go back at least one year of publication). Read also ads, marketing brochures, news bulletins, and subscribe to the publication's newsletter and its Internet blog (participate in their forums and ask questions). Still wanting to learn more? Eliminate some from your industry list and from those that remain, take it a step further.

3. Search for the professional association these industries belong to. Use the Encyclopedia of Associations available online or in any public library. For example, students interested in accounting (as in the professional service industry) can visit the American Institute of Certified Public Accountants at www.aicpa.org. Once on the association page, look to see what informational material, programs, or training they have for students interested in the industry. Usually this information is found on the career tab of the site's home page. See also what conferences, conventions, trade shows, and seminars you can attend. Meet current employees at all levels, from CEO down, and visit booths to collect informational material. Networking starts here (see section on Networking). After all this is done, ask yourself, again: which of these industries am I still interested in? As you answer this question, some industries will be crossed out, but some will remain.

4. By now you should have a manageable number of possible industries of interest (3 to 5, if not fewer). Now it makes sense to drive around town for an informational interview (see section below with this name). After the informational interviews, decide which of them would you like for a career test drive?

13

5. For those industries that passed the informational interview (a much smaller number of industries by this time), conduct a career test drive, commonly referred to as job shadowing (read section below with this name) and/or volunteer work (if the industry allows for it, such as in the case of the health care industry).

6. Lastly, get an industry of interest confirmation check-out from a certified career coach.

STEP 2 HELPERS - CAREER COACHES

The Finding your Industry of Interest activity can generate an overwhelming amount of indecision, especially when it comes to whether to leave in or eliminate an industry. Therefore, you need to reach out to a career coach. They are the ones with the training and experience to help you succeed in this step. Most students think that career coaching is about helping people find a job when they can't find one on their own. However, their interest inventories assessments, which includes feedback from people who know you well, is the most effective tool available that can help you sort out and interpret all those interesting indicators you collected thus far. Just like when you go to the doctor you must be able to talk about your symptoms and what you feel, there has to be a previous career exposure to give your career coach something to work with. CME makes a distinction between a "cold" interest inventory assessment and a "hot" one. Wouldn't it be easier for a person to decide on a car if he or she had the opportunity to test drive it first? Likewise, in a hot interest inventory assessment, you already possess an industry experience to rely on as you move to the interest assessment questions, while in a cold one there are no previous references other than your own mentally constructed sense of reality (a reality that, because of lack of exposure, can be very far from the truth). In a hot interest inventory assessment, the interest indicators you experienced are verified and confirmed, providing the career coach the information about you that he or she needs to help point you to your industry of interest. Once your industry of interest has been determined, you are going to document it in your Career Worksheet.

NETWORKING

Networking is the act of <u>interacting</u> with individuals who have certain expertise to build relationships that will produce current and future benefits. The benefit this definition is referring to is industry information. For that industry information to get to you, there must be a communication channel already in placed between you and current employees of the industry of interest. CME requires students to make career decision on accurate industry information; therefore, learning about networking is highly encouraged. Constantly ask in your social and family circle if they know somebody you may contact who works in any of the industries you are considering. Update your Network Contact Sheet as you meet people. Here are some questions you can ask your family and friends:

Do you know someone who knows the person I want to see for _____? (Example: name of the industry)

Do you know anyone who works for _____? (Example: name of an employer)

Can you give me the name of the hiring decision maker person for _____? (Example: name of a human resources manager)

NETWORK CONTACT SHEET TEMPLATE

Name	Industry	Employer	E-mail	Phone Number

INFORMATIONAL INTERVIEW

You may want to hold off on informational interviews for Item 5 of Finding your Industry of Interest Activity until after you have learned everything you can from other resources. The objective is to get the answers you could not get anywhere else. Here are some recommendations and sample questions:

1. Be selective with whom you speak to. Try to talk to people well known in the industry who have been successful, preferably the ones who are considered experts in the field, with 10-plus years of experience.
2. Do research on the person you are going to interview. See what you can learn about his or her education and experience. This will give you a better idea of what to ask, and the person will be impressed by the fact that you took time to research them. Search for their professional profile on LinkedIn or on their employer's website.
3. Try to schedule the interview at the individual's actual worksite for an accurate picture of the industry environment.
4. Arrive on time (or up to ten minutes early) for your meeting or make the phone call as scheduled.
5. Do not schedule the meeting for more than 20 minutes.
6. Do not exceed your scheduled meeting time unless the person indicates it is okay to do so.
7. Organize your thoughts before the meeting and plan your follow-up question as appropriate.
8. Ask the most important questions first in case you run out of time.
9. Send a formal thank you note following the interview.

Informational interviews are required on almost every step of the CME Job Aid; the samples below are applicable to Step 2 <u>only</u>.

- What do you see happening in the industry in the next five years?
- What changes are occurring in the industry right now?
- What challenges are facing the industry?
- If you were in my position, how would you go about getting into the industry?
- What next steps do you recommend if I was interested in the industry?
- Is there any specific internship or volunteer work opportunity that you recommend for those interested in the industry? (Talk about the possibility of job shadowing.)
- <u>May I contact you if other questions arise?</u>
- <u>Can you refer me to other people in the industry I could also talk to?</u>

Again, ask questions for which answers are not available on other sources. For example, you don't want to ask for general information that is posted on the company's website. However, you can take this opportunity to verify information you found online or to request clarification on a certain issue about the industry that you don't fully understand. The underlined questions are mandatory, as they establish a network channel for more interviewing as required in the steps to follow.

JOB SHADOWING

Job shadowing is a short-term, unpaid exposure to the actual workplace of an occupation. Here, the student gets to follow an employee through his or her work day. However, the objective of this activity is for the student to learn about the industry they are considering in general terms, <u>not</u> focusing on a specific occupation (Step 5 will deal with specific occupation job shadowing). The focus of job shadowing in Step 2 is for you to gain exposure to the different interactions and processes involved in the daily operation of a business (the overall working environment).

Get information from your high school counselor about job shadowing programs available. If there are any, request the school administration to coordinate this activity. Make sure to get your parents involved if you want something to get done.

JOB SHADOWING WORKSHEET

You may use the worksheet below to organize your findings and give you an idea of what kind of information you need to collect.

Information to be collected	Findings
What are the employer's mission and core values?	
What are the employer's top priorities? Note: This may include new projects, goals and/or initiatives.	
What jobs positions are involved in the daily business operation? What are their roles within the operation and how do they support each other? Look for the following: Who depends on or benefits from each job position? Are there any support roles? (Positions that help keep the organization running smoothly but aren't directly associated with either making or selling a product/service (e.g., administrative assistant, receptionist, etc.)	
Who are the vendors or suppliers that the industry depends on? Note: A vendor is a company that provides a service or a product that is needed in the operation of the business (e.g., office supplies, raw materials, parts suppliers, etc.)	
What equipment, tools, materials, and/or technology are used?	
What are the physical characteristics of the worksite? Examples: Location (e.g., indoors, or outdoors) Work space (e.g., office, shop, laboratory) Atmosphere (e.g., calm versus bustling) Physical conditions (e.g., clean versus dirty) What are the major challenges and problems that the employer is currently facing in the industry? Example: issues affecting the employer's productivity and ability to compete in the industry, etc.	

STEP 2 HELPERS - HIGH SCHOOL COUNSELOR

Once you have determined your industry of interest, you are going to let your high school counselor know. He or she is going to assist you with the selection of classes according to the applicable career cluster. The U.S. Department of Education's 16 Career Clusters provide schools with a way of structuring their curriculum so that students can take classes around a particular professional field or industry. When you select a career cluster from the list below, you learn about that field along with your general academics (i.e., English, mathematics, social studies, and science) and within the context of that career field. Since there are several occupations associated with each cluster, the skills learned are usually transferable from one related occupation to another, if they belong to the same career cluster (e.g., business, management, and administration). Once you select a career cluster, your high school guidance counselor can help you select the elective course that will progress you further in your knowledge of the chosen field. Your ability to make wise course selection within an industry in high school will contribute to your success later in a chosen secondary school (college/vocational school) or even the workforce, since you are going to be building on the foundation of previous knowledge for that particular industry.

1. Agriculture, food and natural resources
2. Architecture and construction
3. Arts, audio/video technology and communications
4. Business, management, and administration
5. Education and training
6. Finance
7. Government and public administration
8. Health science
9. Hospitality and tourism
10. Human services
11. Information technology
12. Law, public safety, and security
13. Manufacturing
14. Marketing, sales, and services
15. Science, technology, engineering, and mathematics
16. Transportation, distribution, and logistics.

RECOMMENDATIONS FOR PARENT INVOLVEMENT

Actively engage with your child during both industry researches. Interest is the motivation to enter into a particular industry; however, there are other factors to consider as well, such as your child's personality and natural abilities. Just because your son enjoys playing video games doesn't necessarily means he is going to become a video game designer. Industry research may reveal that there are many other industry possibilities that post a better match for his or her profile. For example, a video game aficionado with the right combination of natural abilities and personality may develop a very gratifying career in other aspects of the video game/entertainment industry (e.g., marketing, retailing, etc.), as his understanding and appreciation for the product is going to allow him to sell it and promote it effectively. As a parent, you must investigate every interest clue further. Again, just because your daughter likes to play the violin, you are not going to disregard the steps of the CME Job Aid, for she is likely to become a famous performer. There is valuable information in industry research that you can incorporate into your daughter's school selection. For example, there are programs that also train for other aspects of the music/entertainment industry (e.g., marketing, media, technology, management, education, etc.) so your daughter can increase her chances of employment after graduation while perfecting the violin. All these other factors to consider will be covered in more detail in the chapters ahead. In the meantime, check out some of these recommendations, including how to work together with your child's career coach and the distinction between a career and a hobby.

- **Enforce good study habits.** Just because you believe that your child is going to be playing sports professionally, become a video game designer, or a famous violin player, he or she can't be doing these activities all the time. Set a schedule for it and make it clear that whichever route he or she chooses, they will still need good grades.

- **Become involved in your child's school. Either start or support any initiative to connect the school with the local business community.** Here are two suggestions:

  1. Propose a workforce day for speakers representing each local industry to present/demonstrate their product or service.

  2. Develop a business-school partnership between your child's school and a local business to discuss the day-to-day operation and hot employer's topics such as attendance, punctuality, teamwork, customer service skills, and problem solving/critical thinking, etc.

- **Do not be afraid to speak up and make suggestions.** For example, if local industry research and exploration does not generate any possible jobs for your child's interest in arts and history, encourage him or her to pursue these activities as a hobby (e.g., become a volunteer at the local museum.) (See section below.)

Most career-counseling strategies and assessments are based on human values. They ask your child to consider what values are important to him or her to then design a career based on these values. This book does not tap into any specific belief system such as the meaning of work or your child's mission in life. Perceptions about work and life in general do tend to change as people get older (life experiences produce changes in priorities, goals, meaning of work/life, etc.) and they are, at the end, a matter of personal choice and self-opinion. CME believes that a child's life is not fulfilled (as in being happy) or defined by a career unless he or she wants it to be, even though some career counselors affirm that you are what you do for a living. This book aims at employment after graduation, student loan default prevention, and that your child gets to actually use the education you paid for. However, according to experts, career satisfaction is the result of the alignment between the individual's values (a sense of purpose, for example) and the type of work the person does.

Given the importance of an individual's values, CME encourages you, as the career decision overseer of your child, to investigate the assessment tool that is being used, and that both you and your child understand what it is designed to do and measure. CMS recommends career assessments to guide extracurricular activities, educational program selection, and to direct you to the kinds of experiences you need to expose your child to. The overall goal of the collaboration with a career coach is to engage your child's natural abilities with relevant work experiences and educational programs. Keep in mind those values are to be determined at the industry level and not at the occupational level. Why? Because an individual's values, once identified, tend to remain unchanged, just as careers, whereas occupations are constantly changing. Examples of career values to discuss with your child and your child's career coach include:

In what kind of environment would they feel comfortable working?
What kind of people would your child like to be around?
What level of responsibility is he or she willing to take?
How important is it that he or she works for a good cause?
How important is it for him or her to help others or to make a difference in other's people lives?

Now, when it comes to careers vs. hobbies, it is not recommended that you tell a child that a certain activity is not going to take him or her anywhere. Instead, take that activity as a ruling factor for industry elimination. As you go through the industry of interest activity, you are going to help your child identify which industry in the Step 1 list builds on that special interest. In Step 5, CME explains specifically how it is done. However, as a general rule, if nobody is willing to pay for your child to perform a certain task, then that activity is a hobby; but if somebody is willing to pay for this activity, it is a possible career. The best approach to guide your child to the path that leads to employment is to understand your role as a parent, within CME. You are a career facilitator whose job is to provide the exposure and experience so that the answer to whether their interest is a possible career or a hobby does not come from you but from your child. Being a career facilitator means that you are going to make time in your busy schedule to expose your child to the actual work field of whatever they are interested in. You are going to take them to talk to real people who have chosen that path so they can see and hear with their own eyes and ears what they'll end up doing and what they have to say about it. Always be open and flexible. Consider the following examples:

- Interest in fashion may lead to occupations in the retail industry such as merchandiser, sales representative, buyer, fashion coordinator, designer, etc.
- Interest in music may find demand for jobs in the technical, marketing, or management aspects of the music industry and not necessarily only a performer.
- Interest in sports can lead to careers within the sports industry such as administration, finance, marketing, sales, manufacturing, coaching, sports medicine, etc.

– NOTES –

CHAPTER 3
WHO ARE THE EMPLOYERS IN THIS INDUSTRY? (STEP 3)

Tailoring cannot begin until you meet the client and take his or measurements, and so is the case with career planning. To learn the skills that employers are looking for, you need to find out who they are in the first place. Therefore, in the search box of any of the search engines or business directories listed in the activity below, type the service or product that your industry of interest is known for (e.g., accounting, or legal services, banks, doctor's office, etc.); then, select your city/area and click the search button. You may also use the industry name as per the NAICS classification or phrases that include the name of the service and the area combined (e.g., accounting firms in Miami-Dade County, or auto shops in zip code 33165). Once the Employer List Activity is completed, you may proceed to Step 4. Here are two examples:

Employer Name	Contact Information (website, phone, address)	Contact Person (job title, phone, e-mail)	Employer Description (who they are and what they do)
Brown & Brown Accounting Services	www.brownandbrowntax.com Phone: 555-555-5555 Address: 12345 SW 158 Ave. Miami, Florida 33125	John White - Human Resources manager Phone: 305 555-5555 Ext 123 E-mail: john@brownandbrown.com	Large tax preparation company with offices in all 50 states and overseas. Offers banking, payroll, personal finance, and business consulting services.
Smith & Company, P.A.	(No website) Phone: 888-888-8888 Address: 6789 SW 222 Ave. Miami, Florida 33125	Joe Black - Office manager. Phone: 888-888-8888 Ext. 345 E-mail: Joe@smithandcompany.com	Small accounting firm serving the West Miami area. Offers income tax preparation for businesses and individuals, as well as bookkeeping and payroll services.

Note: These two examples are based on Accounting, Tax Preparation, Bookkeeping, and Payroll Services (NAICS 5412) as the Industry of Interest.

EMPLOYER LIST ACTIVITY

Instructions: Keep the number of employers to a manageable number. For example, if there are more than 100 accounting firms in your area, contact 10 to 20 of them. Start with the ones closer to you, working yourself out until you reach the one hour of commuting radius. Use online business directories and search engines such as: http://www.google.com; http://local.yahoo.com; http://www.bing.com/businessportal; http://www.yellowpages.com; http://www.yelp.com; and http://manta.com.

– NOTES –

CHAPTER 4
WHAT JOBS DO THESE EMPLOYERS NEED TO FILL? (STEP 4)

To get an accurate answer, you are going to have to ask the employers themselves. They are the ones who really know what jobs need to get filled and what qualifications are required. In Step 4, you are going to research each employer recorded in Step 3's Employer list. CME calls it "inside research."

Employer inside research has three objectives. First is to find out what jobs are involved in an employer's daily operation; second, what their tasks are, and third, what their corresponding qualifications are. In this step, you and your parents are required to complete the Job List Activity, which captures all three of them. Here are some examples for you to have an idea of what it could look like.

Employer: Brown & Brown Accounting Services

Column # 1	Column # 2	Column # 3
Job Position	**Tasks**	**Qualifications** **(Education, Skills, and Experience)**
Certified Public Accountant	• Complete income tax returns for individual clients and small businesses. • Audit clients' financial records for IRS compliance. • Create and analyze budgets. • Recommend methods to save money. • Increase client retention.	**Education** • Bachelor Degree in Accounting • CPA Certified **Skills:** • Strong verbal and written communication skills. • Attention to details. • Customer service skills. **Experience** Minimum of **1 year** of experience
Bookkeeper	• Monitor office supply levels and reorder as necessary • Pay vendor invoices • Issue invoices to customers • Collect sales taxes from customer sales and remit them to the government • Ensure that receivables are collected • Record cash receipts and make money deposits • Conduct a monthly reconciliation of bank accounts to ensure their accuracy • Maintain the petty cash fund • Maintain an accounting filing system • Maintain the annual budget • Calculate variances from the budget and report significant issues to leadership • Comply with local, state, and federal government reporting requirements • Process payroll • Provide clerical and administrative support	**Education** • QuickBooks® trained and certified • Coursework in accounting or business-related studies • High school diploma • Microsoft Office certified **Skills** • PC data entry and 10-key calculator skills • Knowledge of the bookkeeping/payroll software • Ability to work under strict deadlines, while organizing multiple projects at the same time. • Knowledge of applicable local, state, and federal wage and hour laws. **Experience:** • 2+ years of experience in bookkeeping services to include payroll, general ledgers, and financial statements

| Client Services | • Greet incoming clients in a personalized and inviting manner
• Schedule clients with a tax professional
• Maintain clean and organized office | **Education**
• High school diploma

Skills
• Strong customer service skills
• Strong organizational and time-management skills.
• Knowledge of cash registration operations
• Knowledge and experience with Microsoft Office

Experience
No prior experience required |

Employer: Smith & Company, P.A.

Job Position	Tasks	Education, Skills, and Experience (Qualifications)
Payroll Technician	• Enter, verify, and process employee time and attendance records using the time and attendance payroll system. • Process employee data changes • Deliver instruction/training to employees regarding the use of payroll-related systems including clocking in and out, and online access of pay stub.	**Education** • High school diploma • Related post-secondary coursework • Microsoft Office trained and certified - Excel knowledge at the advanced level. **Skills** • Strong quantitative and analytical thinking skills • Attention to detail and thoroughness **Experience** • 2+ recent years of payroll processing experience

JOB LIST ACTIVITY

Instruction: The goal of this activity is to list <u>all possible job positions/occupations</u> involved in the employer's daily operation. You don't have to repeat the same thing over and over if it has already been recorded. In the example above, Brown & Brown Accounting Services shows Certified Public Accountant, Bookkeeper, and Client Services; whereas for Smith & Company, P.A. only the Payroll Technician position was recorded. This is because, even though Smith & Company, P.A. was also looking for a bookkeeper and an accountant, we only documented the position we did not have. **<u>When job positions start showing up over and over again and no new positions come out, stop and proceed to Step 5.</u>** To complete the Job List Activity, first start with the employer's official website. This information can be located in the contact information column of your Employer List. Once on the website, look for the Careers or Jobs tab. If available, subscribe to the employer's job alerts. This service sends you an e-mail notification every time there is an opening. If there is no career tab on the website, your next option is online research. Chances are you may already have a good idea of all possible jobs from the activities in the previous steps (e.g., reading industry publications, job shadowing, informational interview, etc.). So, all you have to do is search these jobs in search engines such as www.monster.com or www.careerbuilder. com. Once in the job listing, you can find the rest of the information you need to fill out the tasks and qualifications column. The last step is to conduct an informational interview with the individual you identified as your contact person in your Employer List. The purpose of the Informational Interview in Step 4 is to find out if there is any other additional information about qualifications that were not mentioned in the job posting but that are important to the employer. Sample questions for this activity include:

- What personality traits, special abilities, and skills fit best for this position?
- What makes some people successful at this job and others less so?
- What kind of attitude or qualities do they demonstrate?

These questions are designed to reveal what employers are really looking for in their candidates. The skills you commonly hear in informational interviews that are not always mentioned in job announcement posts include:

- **Accountability** (accepts responsibility for actions taken and keeps others informed of their outcomes)
- **Initiative** (identifies what needs to be done and takes action without being asked)
- **Problem Solving Skills/Critical thinking skills** (breaks down problems and considers all possible solutions)
- **Adaptability and Flexibility** (being open to change)

- **Teamwork** (promotes cooperation and commitment within a team to achieve goals)
- **Interpersonal Skills** (interacts well with others at work to include the ability to deal with conflict effectively)

Record your findings in the qualification column and don't forget to select electives courses that teach any of the skills mentioned on the job openings (e.g., Microsoft Office, Advance Excel, QuickBooks, etc.)

– NOTES –

CHAPTER 5
TO WHICH OF THESE JOBS CAN I CONTRIBUTE THE MOST? (STEP 5)

Let's begin this chapter explaining the significance of the two underlined words in the question. *Jobs* refers to a group of tasks that employers need to cover in order to conduct business. The second word refers to an individual *contribution* to the employer's final product or service. Simply put, the objective of Step 5 is to figure out on which of the jobs listed in Step 4 you can be more useful to the employer. The job you contribute to the most is the one where you are able to meet its educational requirements and where your natural skills can be put to the most productive use for the benefit of your employer.

Having said this, direct your attention to the job list you created in Step 4 and take a closer look at column #3. Notice how a job qualification is made up of three components: Education, Skills, and Experience. Step 5 looks at the first two components: Education and Skills. To answer Step 5's question, you are going to perform two sweeps through Step 4's job list. In the first sweep, you are going to eliminate the job position that requires an education you are not willing to pursue. This is called the *Educational Path Decision*. Then, from the jobs that remain, you are going to identify the ones whose tasks build upon your unique skills and aptitudes. This final sweep is called the *Tasks-Skills Match*.

Have you ever heard the phrase "no pain, no gain"? Well, CME uses a similar phrase; it is called "no paper, no job." *Paper* refers to a degree, certification, or license that shows that you have met the education requirement for the job. For example, if the job opening specifically states that only candidates with a bachelor's degree in accounting will be considered, and you don't have that piece of paper that prove that you have a bachelor's degree in accounting, you simply can't get the job. Therefore, as you look at each job's educational requirement, you are going to decide which position's educational path you are willing to commit to. There are four possible paths to decide from: the 4-year university path, the community college path, the vocational school path, and the apprenticeship path.

The 4-year university path: The 4-year university path is a bachelor degree program awarded by a university. These programs require 120 to 128 credits, although you can transfer up to 60 college credits from a community college. Bachelor's degrees consist of general education courses and electives in addition to the specific subject of study required courses, the "major." There are two types of bachelor's degrees; the Bachelor of Arts (BA) and the Bachelor of Science (BS). The BA requires you to take the majority of your courses in the liberal arts (e.g., language, literature, and humanities). The BS, on the other hand, requires you to take the majority of your courses in science (e.g., physics, chemistry, and mathematics).

The community college path: Community colleges are two-year schools that provide affordable post-secondary education as a pathway to a four-year degree. Most community colleges have what is called articulation of agreement. An articulation of agreement facilitates the transfer of college credits among state-assisted institutions so that students can continue to make progress toward their bachelor degree at a university. For example, some community colleges have agreements with their state universities that permit graduates of parallel programs to transfer with a junior standing. When considering this route, find out the credit transfer requirements of the university you want to attend. Also, some community colleges develop partnerships with local businesses to offer technical or vocational training tailored to their industries. Some of these training programs lead to job placement. This means that if this path is chosen, you could be fully trained for the workforce in an average of six months to a year. These programs are called professional certification programs. Examples include:

Biotechnology: Biotechnology programs seek to prepare students for immediate entry-level employment in the biotechnology, pharmaceutical, or medical device manufacturing industry.

Banking Specialist: These programs provide general knowledge and technical skills that establish a financial services career. The certificate includes career entry employees with clerical, administrative, or customer service tasks. Positions available under this program include customer service representative and financial/banking specialist. This program also meets the requirements for the Center for Financial Training national industry diploma.

Accounting Technology Management: The Accounting Applications College Credit Certificate programs prepare students for employment as accounting clerks, data processing clerks, junior accountants, and assistant accountants, or to provide supplemental training for persons previously or currently employed in these occupations. The curriculum teaches students the principles, procedures, and theories of organizing and maintaining business and financial records, and the preparation of accompanying financial reports.

Air Cargo Management: The Air Cargo Management College Credit Certificate program gives students the skills required to gain employment as an air cargo agent. These programs are usually completed in one or two semesters. Earned credits can be applied towards an Associate in Science degree in Aviation Administration.

The vocational school path: Vocational schools, also called trade schools, are post-secondary learning institutions that specialize in providing students with the technical skills they need to perform the tasks of a particular job within a certain industry. The duration of this program usually ranges from six months to a year. Examples of vocational schools include:

- Culinary schools
- Beauty and cosmetology schools
- Health care vocational schools that offer training for medical assistant technician, medical front office and billing, and <u>patient care technician</u>

The apprenticeship path: An apprenticeship is a program where the students learn a skilled trade through classroom work and on-the-job training at the same time. A student completing an apprenticeship program becomes a journeyperson (skilled craftsperson) in that trade. Most programs require a high school diploma or the completion of certain course work and/or may include other specific requirements, such as passing certain aptitude tests, proof of physical ability to perform the duties of the trade, and the possession of a valid driver's license. Since students are trained in the actual workplace and receive a salary, the program entrance process is like applying for a job. Apprenticeship programs prepare successful graduates to work as journeymen in the areas of electrical, fire sprinkler, air conditioning, refrigeration, heating, plumbing, sheet metal, and many other trades.

EDUCATIONAL PATH ACTIVITY

Instructions: Add a 4th column to Step 4's job list as in the examples provided and name it Educational Path. Seek the assistance of an admission advisor or counselor from a local post-secondary school (e.g., college advisor or an admission representative). The information to be collected should include:

- Applicable post-secondary educational path
- Admission requirements for the post-secondary program (What it takes to get in, e.g., admission tests and GPA)
- Program's graduation requirements (What it takes to finish e.g., duration of the program, amount of credits required, difficulty level, etc.)

Required educational path is usually listed in the actual job posting under qualifications (Refer to examples). Otherwise, do some inside research on your own to find out the employer's desired education path for the job (e.g., bachelor, associate, certification, etc.). Once you have this information, you are going to contact a school advisor or counselor from the applicable post-secondary institution to gather the rest of the information, as in the example on the next page.

Job Position: Registered Nurse

Tasks	Qualifications	Educational Path
	Education, Skills, and Experience	
Tasks • Administer medications to patients and monitor for side effects. • Record medical information and vital signs. • Consult and coordinate with team members to assess, plan, implement, or evaluate patient care plans.	**Education** • Graduate of an accredited school of nursing • Bachelor of Science in Nursing (BSN) • Must be licensed in the State of Florida as a Registered Nurse (RN) **Skills** • Technical skills • Communication • Critical thinking • Interpersonal skills • Flexibility • Organizational skills • Professional accountability **Experience** One year of experience in hospital setting.	Bachelor of Science in Nursing (BSN) • Completion of a minimum of 43 credit hours • GPA of 3.60 in all attempted college course work • Maintain consistent advisement in the Department of Nursing for a minimum of one year prior to the application deadline • Pass Florida Registered Nurse (RN) Exam

After you get a good idea of what it takes to get in each of the programs and what it takes to graduate, go ahead and cross out the jobs with a path you are <u>not</u> willing to commit to. The jobs that remain will continue to the last sweep, the tasks-skills match activity.

STEP 5 HELPERS - HIGH SCHOOL COUNSELOR AND TEACHERS

As you can see, each job listed points out to one specific educational path to be an eligible candidate (e.g., bachelor's degree, professional certifications, licenses, etc.). To assist you in making this decision, your **high school counselor, and teachers** first asses your overall high school performance, then make recommendations as to the type, difficulty level, and duration of the academic program in which you are most likely to succeed (e.g., a 2-year vocational school curriculum versus a 4-year college curriculum). However, this does <u>not</u> mean that because a student has failing grades in certain academic areas he or she <u>should not consider</u> a 4-year university path. It simply means that this student will have to commit to work hard to bring his or her academic performance up to college level. Therefore, the issue to consider here is not how smart you are, but how hard you are willing to work. <u>It is about commitment and motivation and has nothing to do with a student's potential</u>. The question to ask at this point is: To which of these four educational paths am I <u>willing</u> to commit? This is something only you can answer. Be honest with yourself, your parents, and your teachers.

Do not stress too much about this. When you make an educational path decision you are not making a <u>permanent career decision</u> like you did in Step 2 when you decided what industry you were going to be part of. Here, you are just deciding what is going to be your <u>first role or function</u> within the career that you have already chosen. Can you change an occupation within an industry later? Of course, you can. Most likely you will anyway, whether you like it or not. There will be future changes within the industry outside your control. In fact, you will be forced to continue your education just for the sake of staying employed.

TASKS-SKILLS MATCH ACTIVITY

In this activity, you are going to focus on the <u>results or outcome</u> that your natural skills and personality type are most likely to produce. Employers look for candidates who have the potential of bringing a <u>benefit</u> to their organization (e.g., increase sales, bring improvement to service quality, etc.). Therefore, a good match between a task and an identified natural skill/personality type can positively affect an individual's results at a given task. Here is an example of how it works:

Outcome: Generated
20 new accounts
versus 5 from the
previous quarter

Job Task: Deliver product
presentation to group of clients

Natural Skill: verbal/linguistic abilities - Social
Personality type

Notice how in this example, the individual's natural skill, combined with his or her personality type, formed the foundation for the result he or she was able to achieve (20 new accounts brought to the employer versus 5 on the previous presentation by another employee). In this same way, a well-defined base (a skill/ natural ability, personality type, and job task match) can determine your contribution to the employer (e.g., solve a problem that nobody was able to find a solution for or bring an improvement to a product or service). Given the importance of these underlying traits, identifying your natural skills and personality type combination is the <u>key factor</u> for a successful job match. A natural ability is a special facility for performing a certain task. The more accurately you can identify those natural abilities, the more effectively you can identify the jobs or occupations that build on those unique abilities.

Why is this task/natural ability match so important? The answer, again, is value. As mentioned earlier, employers look for candidates whose skills represent a gain to their business. In the example provided, the value is represented by the 20 new accounts this individual was able to bring on board because of his or her skills. A proper match between a natural ability, a personality type, and a skill increases the chances for the kind of <u>results that an employer can benefit from</u>. In fact, people do tend to excel at tasks that align with their natural abilities, personality type and interest.

To complete the Tasks-Skills Match Activity, you are going to have to work closely with a career coach. Under their guidance, you are going to determine which of the remaining jobs your natural abilities/personality type could have the most impact on. Traditionally, the job of career coaches has been to assess students' natural abilities, work environment preferences, personality, and values to recommend a possible career fit. However, in the midst of finding out what students like to do, employers' needs are often ignored. To prevent this, the objective of career coaches is to identify and match your unique abilities and strengths with the job's tasks. This is why the question posted on this step is worded: to which of these positions can I contribute the most? This stresses the importance of moving from a self-centered approach (what I enjoy and makes me happy) to an employer value-based approach (how well I can do what the employer needs to be done).

The current students' self-centered approach to career coaching does not solve the problem of new graduates' unemployment and degree utilization, which is the goal of this book. Besides the interest inventories you learned in Chapter 2, career coaches utilize personality assessments and accomplishments exercises that can help you identify the unique abilities you possess, and give you specific recommendations as to what jobs on the updated list would fit your profile.

The objective of the career coach is to get to the very basics of your natural abilities and unique personality traits to match them to the tasks where they can be put to the most productive use. Once this is determined, you should be able to identify the job where you can make the most impact. This is the job that will be documented in your career worksheet. Prior to contacting your career coach, make sure to complete the Step 5 shadowing activity on the next page.

STEP 5: JOB SHADOWING ACTIVITY

There are three pieces of information you need to give your career coach in order for them to help you in the Tasks-Skills Match Activity: your industry of interest, your updated job list (jobs that remained after the educational path activity), and a record of the occupational indicators you have observed. The first two pieces of information you should already have; therefore, the purpose of job shadowing in this step is to collect occupational indicators for your career coach to analyze. During the first field exploration, the focus was on interest, and you were looking at the broad aspects of industries. In this activity, career exploration is narrowed down to the occupations listed on your updated job list, which means that, this time, you are going to be paying close attention to the day-to-day tasks being performed by each job (use your employer list contacts from Step 3). As you conduct the job shadowing, ask yourself question such as:

- What tasks seem to come easy to you? For example, when given the opportunity during the job shadowing, you demonstrated a natural ability for handling certain precision tools with great accuracy.
- What tasks required a skill for which you have received praise from your teachers? For example, a job position requires oral presentation of a product to prospective clients, and you have repeatedly received praise from your speech teacher for your oral presentations in class.
- Was there any position that involved a task for which, when performed in other settings, you seemed to lose track of time and didn't want anyone or anything to disturb you? For example, a position that involved fixing engines, and in your free time you like to buy old cars and work on their engines.
- Was there any job that involved a task for which you, your friends, and/or family members have repeatedly said you are good at? For example, a job position that requires fixing computers, and friends/family members are always coming to you with issues with their computer.

Other Resources

You may take the Armed Services Vocational Aptitude Battery (ASVAB) sponsored by the Department of Defense to help you identify interests, abilities, and personal preferences. This assessment consists of nine short tests covering word knowledge, paragraph comprehension, arithmetic reasoning, mathematics knowledge, general science, auto and shop information, mechanical comprehension, electronics information, and assembling objects. Scores are provided on a report called the ASVAB Student Result Sheet (usually within thirty days) together with a copy of *The ASVAB Workbook*, which explains ASVAB results and how to match the student's profile to 250 civilian and military occupations. Since composite scores measure the student's aptitude/capacity for handling more advanced academic training, a certain amount of preparation is required to achieve the best possible results. Achieving a maximum score increases vocational opportunities, as the armed forces use the ASVAB results to determine not only the individual's qualifications for enlistment, but also for determining the types of jobs and training for which the person is best suited. The ASVAB can be taken any time after the tenth grade and scores are good for two years; however, sophomore scores are not accepted for enlistment. **Taking the ASVAB does not obligate a student to join the military.**

– NOTES –

CHAPTER 6
WHICH IS THE BEST SCHOOL TO TRAIN FOR THIS JOB?
(STEP 6)

Step 5 completed the process of getting to know your future employers and what they are looking for so tailoring can begin. As this question implies, career tailoring starts with training, which refers to post-secondary education (secondary education being high school or college prep school). Let's begin this chapter by establishing that, education, when done correctly, is an investment. An investment, by definition, is the purchase of something with the hope of that it will generate income in the future. CME's Job Aid is an educational investing tool as it allows the investor-student to understand what kind of training is going to be <u>purchased</u> and what specific <u>purpose</u> it is going to serve. Therefore, the question to answer in this step is: Which is the best school to train for this position? (Referring to the job position recorded on your Career Worksheet). Chapter 6 establishes the criteria for choosing a post-secondary school program <u>based on the recommendation from people who are already in the industry and their employers.</u>

This step is a straightforward process; go to for the position you selected in Step 5 and see what degree, certification, or licenses the employer is looking for, as stated on an actual job posting. Once this is determined, you are going to look for the school that provides the training for that degree, certification, or professional license. But, how do you know which school is best? CME is going to tell you what questions to ask and how to compare 'apples to apples' to determine which school option is going to make you competitive in the job market when you graduate. It is called the CME School Test.

The following questions apply to employers or current employees in the industry. Use the employer list you created on Step 3 to contact the right people and review recommendations for informational interviews provided in the previous steps.

1. Do you recommend any particular school to train for this position?

    Note: Look at employees' profiles (LinkedIn or on the employer's website) and find out where they went to school.

2. (If applicable to the position) Do you know of any school that offers _____ license/certification?

    Note: This may include the school that offers pre-licensing courses.

3. Do you recruit job candidates from any particular school?

4. Do you know of any school or professor that has earned awards or special recognition within the industry?

   Note: This may also be a professor that is well recognized in the industry and that is known for bringing industry issues and challenges as projects to the classroom.

5. Do you have an internship agreement with any particular school?

   Notes: An internship may be required as part of a major, such as in the case of health care occupations (e.g., nurses, physicians, etc.). But it also applies to apprenticeship programs and vocational schools (e.g., a culinary school having a special relation with an industry-known hotel or restaurant chain).

The following questions apply to students' counselors/advisors for the institutions being considered. Prior to visiting the schools, consider the following recommendations:

- Visit the school website prior to the meeting. With the above questions in mind, conduct online research first, narrowing your choices to a manageable list (5 to 10 maybe); then, contact the school counselor or student advisor. Some answers such as the one about extracurricular activity opportunities can be researched online.
- Ask only the questions for which you still need answers. (Some questions may have already been addressed online.)
- Request a meeting with a professor in your major/program.
- Be prepared to answer questions about yourself and about your career goals.
- Ask questions about the background and experiences of the professors you meet.

Then, ask the following questions:

1. What employers are known for recruiting from the school?

   Note: Review the school placement statistics to look at the percentage of graduates placed within a certain period of time upon graduation, and for which organizations. Ask the school where to find this information.

2. Is the school accredited and certified by my industry of interest?

   Note: Accreditation is the recognition of a post-secondary educational institution by a regional or national organization, which indicates that the school has met its objectives and is maintaining prescribed educational standards. Specialized accreditation of a given individual program is granted by professional organizations to ensure that the program meets the requirements established by the industry. Professional fields that require occupational licenses issued by the state required students to complete pre-license courses from an accredited institution as qualification for licensure/certification.

3. Has the school or any of the professors in the program earned any awards or special recognition within the industry?

4. Does the school have an internship agreement with any particular employer?

5. If applicable, does the school offer any national licensing/certification after graduation?

CME SCHOOL TEST

Instructions: Write the name of the schools being considered on the chart below to compare them. Then, answer questions based on information collected from employers' representatives and post-secondary school student counselors. You may add more columns as necessary. The schools with the most 'Yes' <u>may</u> indicate the best option for training, and may be the school that will be recorded on your career worksheet. However, this is a team decision that may include other factors specific to your own situation. The team includes your parents, high school counselor, and career coach.

Test Questions	School 1 Name:		School 2 Name:		School 3 Name:	
	Yes	No	Yes	No	Yes	No
Is the school accredited and certified by my selected industry professional association?	☐	☐	☐	☐	☐	☐
Does the school have a strong academic program for my selected major? Is it widely recognized in the industry and recommended by current employees?	☐	☐	☐	☐	☐	☐
Do my listed employers in Step 3 recruit from this school?	☐	☐	☐	☐	☐	☐
Has the school or any or its professors earned any awards or special recognition within the industry?	☐	☐	☐	☐	☐	☐
Does the school have an internship agreement with a known employer in the industry?	☐	☐	☐	☐	☐	☐
If applicable, does the school offer any national licensing/certification after graduation?	☐	☐	☐	☐	☐	☐
Does the location of the school affect extracurricular activity opportunities such as part-time jobs, internships, and volunteer work? For example, for engineering majors, a school located in an industrial area may offer more relevant extracurricular opportunities than a college town surrounded by a few small businesses, or a culinary student may have more opportunities in a tourism-based local economy than in a farming town's school.	☐	☐	☐	☐	☐	☐

STEP 6 HELPERS - POST-SECONDARY SCHOOL COUNSELORS

The student counselor's job is to explain a program's objectives and a description of the courses you will be taking. They are also responsible for guiding you through the admission process. Once this information is collected, it is going to be distributed as follows. The program's curriculum information (e.g., course descriptions and objectives) is going to go to your career coach, and the admission requirements will go to your high school counselor.

STEP 6 HELPERS - CAREER COACHES

Your career coach is going to receive the program curriculum information and is going to compare it to the job's tasks listed in the worksheet. Then, he or she is going to confirm whether the program you are considering will give you the knowledge and skills you need to perform those tasks (including professional licensing and state certifications). This is usually the process for a vocational school path and for the apprenticeship path. However, the college path (whether it is the traditional 4-year or community college) could get a little complicated, if it is not stated by the employer in the job posting. For example, if the job listed in your worksheet says that a BS in accounting is required, then your major is going to be accounting. But, if not specifically stated, then your career coach needs to look up the job's tasks to help you decide on a major that will provide the training you need. For example, if the tasks being performed in the position rely heavily on report writing, oral presentations, or in-depth mathematics, you may see your career coach recommending a certain major. **The idea is that he or she is going to use the actual job's tasks as a guide for your major, minors, and elective courses, including current employees' input/insights collected during the different informational interviews you conducted in the previous steps.**

A *major* is a concentration of specialized courses, usually a minimum of 24 credit hours taken during the third and fourth years in of a 4-year college program. They constitute the specific requirements you must complete to get a bachelor's degree (which is what employers want to see). These academic requirements are designed so that you gain in-depth knowledge of a particular subject. Generally, the subject that is the focus of the major is the same as the department offering the major (e.g., accounting, English, chemistry, psychology, etc.), although there are majors that have requirements from other departments for a wider understanding of the subject. For example, physics majors may have to take courses in the mathematics department, allowing the student to concentrate on a certain area of the industry. This is why within a major, you also have a concentration. A *concentration* is when, within the chosen major, you select courses that emphasize a particular aspect of the field. For example, a business major student may specialize in the international aspect of business as opposed to domestic. Concentration may also lead you to take courses in other departments/fields. For example, an economics major who wishes to concentrate on econometrics (the application of mathematics, statistical methods, and computer science to economic data) may need to take courses offered by the mathematics and computer science departments; whereas one who wishes to concentrate in applied economics may need to take business courses. Besides majors there are three other important definitions to understand. They are minors, double majors, and electives. You have a minor when you take a set of required courses in a particular subject but in a fewer amount than in a major. However, your transcript will demonstrate some in-depth knowledge in that second subject. A double major is when students complete the requirements for two majors simultaneously. Most majors allow students to choose courses freely (not necessarily related to the field), called electives. Here is when the student may be able to satisfy the requirements for both. Keep in mind, however, that CME discourages the use of course electives as a means of career exploration. You don't need to waste a whole semester that could have been used to gain an employable skill and spend thousands of dollars to explore a subject when there are other more effective and less expensive means available. (Refer back to industry research in Step 2.)

STEP 6 HELPERS - HIGH SCHOOL COUNSELORS

Your high school counselor is going to receive the program curriculum information, admission requirements, and job tasks to plan your school year accordingly. For instance, he or she may recommend the classes that would prepare you to get admitted by the school (e.g., certain prerequisite courses or a certain academic level for a given subject). In addition, he or she may recommend the elective classes and extracurricular activities you can take that would give the skills/knowledge to perform job's tasks. Example of classes that you can take within the high school curriculum may include foreign languages, computer technology classes, speech/drama classes, etc. Also, based on the job's tasks, the counselor can show you what extracurricular activities are available in the school that will give you experience at those tasks. For example, for a job that depends on writing skills, the counselor might recommend the student join the school's newspaper club, or for an accounting major may advise the student to join a club as the treasurer.

– NOTES –

CHAPTER 7
WOULD I HAVE WORK EXPERIENCE FOR THIS JOB WHEN I GRADUATE? IF NOT, WHERE WOULD I GO TO GET THE EXPERIENCE I NEED? (STEP 7)

By this time, the education requirement should have been put in motion by choosing the best place to get trained. What's left to tailor is experience. In this step, you will learn how to determine if you will have work experience when you graduate and if not, where to get it. To answer this question there are two things you need to know. First, you need to understand what employers perceive as work experience and second, you need to know how determine if both the educational requirements and work experience can be gained simultaneously within your chosen school's program.

For employers, work experience can only be counted if the tasks they listed on the job posting were performed in a context similar to the one provided by the job being filled. *Context* refers to a physical place, time frame, and a job title under which the skills you learned in class were applied. For example, a school might give a student a diploma that says he or she has a Bachelor's in Accounting, but if there is no context where the student actually performed accounting work it is almost like he or she does not have the skills, even though there is a piece of paper that says so. This explains why some recent colleges' graduates end up in entry level jobs that only require a high school diploma.

For the purpose of an employer's perception, let's establish that both the experience and educational requirement can be obtained together if the program's curriculum includes on-the-job training. Programs that include on-the-job training in their curriculum are those that require an **internship** as part of their graduation requirements and those in the **apprentice path. Internships** can be applicable to both the vocational school path and the college path (whether it is the traditional 4-year university or community college). For example, internships are required for most occupations in the health care industry (e.g., nurses, doctors, etc.) but they are not exclusive for this industry (e.g., a culinary school may also require an internship, as well). What is important is that internships give you the opportunity to take what is learned in the classroom and apply it to a real work context. Under these programs, interns have a supervisor/teacher who assigns specific tasks and evaluates the student's overall performance in the actual work setting (e.g., a hospital with real patients or a restaurant with real customers). When internship is a graduation requirement, it usually takes place towards the end of the program and it is arranged by the school.

Apprentice programs, on the other hand, are a combination of on-the-job training and classroom instruction in which the students learn the practical and theoretical aspects of certain occupations simultaneously. Benefits of apprentice programs may include:

- Salaries that increase as the student learns the skill.
- On-the-job experience and national certifications already included in the program.
- Students receive an education paid by the employer.
- Receive permanent employment by the same institution where training was received.

There are many different types of apprentice programs, but the most common is the armed forces. The armed forces combine on-the-job training and work experience for just about any civilian occupation found in the job market. Also, the government pays a large percentage of the post-secondary school tuition for the academic requirements of such occupations (may pay up to 75% of tuition for full-time, active-duty enlistees). Through the armed forces, the student work experience is validated by a prestigious institution. Despite these benefits, joining the military is a privilege, and the decision for this option must be founded on a conscious and genuine appreciation for its core values and mission. It is a commitment to an unconditional service to our nation, and not to get college paid for. If the military option aligns with your personal belief, and if you have given serious thought to the reason to join, then industry exploration and employer research should focus on what branch of service will offer the training and experience you need for the jobs in demand within your industry of interest (e.g., many commercial airline pilots come from the air force or the navy and so do their aircraft mechanics).

Nevertheless, to make the determination as to whether you are going to have work experience, you need to ask the student counselor from the institution you chose in Step 6 to explain in detail the program's curriculum. If you are not on the apprentice path and an internship is not a graduation requirement, most likely you are not going to have experience when you graduate. This means that you are responsible for getting real work experience on your own. There are ways you can do this: an internship (sought on your own), a part-time job, volunteer work, and/other any other specific extracurricular activity.

INTERNSHIPS

Since an internship may lead to full-time employment after graduation, the application-acceptance process is similar to applying for a job. Both paid and unpaid internships can be applied for through a post-secondary school career center, the employer official's website, and/or contacting the employer directly. (Contact the ones in your employer list first).

PART-TIME JOBS

Part-time jobs provide the opportunity for students to develop what is known as soft skills. When references are contacted, employers inquire about the applicant's soft skills, which is also the primary purpose of a job interview. Employers tend to avoid candidates who lack these soft skills, even if they possess strong technical knowledge. Soft skills include:

- Interpersonal skills, (e.g., how successfully you interact with managers and coworkers or being able to recall a time when you had a difficult coworker as part of your team and how you were able to handle it).
- Communication skills, (e.g., being able to tell about a time when you had to use your presentation skills to influence someone's opinion). They may ask, "Describe the most difficult or complex idea, situation, or process you ever had to explain to a supervisor or team member."
- Integrity (e.g., being able to tell about a time when your integrity was challenged and how you handled it).
- Initiative (e.g., taking tasks that are not part of your job description).
- Leadership (e.g., knowing how to deal with resistance when decisions are made).
- Adaptability (e.g., being able to adapt to a management directive with which you do not agree).
- Decisiveness (e.g., facing unexpected situations with a positive attitude).
- Independence (e.g., completing a task on your own with no supervision).

Moreover, since the United States is in general a customer-service-based economy, seek part-time jobs that require you to deal directly with the public (e.g., dealing with difficult customers, answering phone inquiries, handling complaints, and sales).

VOLUNTEER WORK EXAMPLES

- Volunteer at a parks and recreation department.
- Volunteer at a hospital/clinic.
- Get involved with organizations that deal with the environment, such as recycling programs and beautification efforts in the community.
- Get involved in organizations that deal with social problems such as drugs, alcohol, and crime.
- Get involved with organizations that provide services for the homeless.
- Tutor younger kids in school subjects.
- Get involved in church projects.

Overall, extracurricular activities and academics go hand in hand. When the students have been exposed to the real world and understand the relevancy of academic skills being learned in class, they tend to stay focused and motivated. For example, a student interested in the health service industry should seek volunteer work in a medical facility where he or she can be exposed to a variety of occupations available in this field and learn about the training pathways into these jobs. Working in a hospital, such as in this case, also gives students access to health professionals, who themselves can offer advice and information about the industry and in some instances become their professional mentors.

CME encourage involvement in extracurricular activities as early as the 9th grade (see high school checklist) so in the later grades students can obtain leadership positions. This kind of experience can become a decisive admission factor when applying to competitive schools, internships, scholarships, and full-time employment. For example, a student who in the 9th grade becomes involved in a community club may get to achieve a key position by 12th grade and look at all the things that he or she is going to be able to document as experience:

- Defined and communicated project goals to a student committee of **50** members (communication skills).
- Anticipated and planned for any challenge that may have prevented the project goals from being achieved (leadership skills).
- Distributed tasks to team members (leadership skills).
- Ensured the team members had the tools and supplies necessary to achieve the projects' goals on schedule and within budget (leadership skills).
- Conducted weekly briefings to a committee of **30** students (oral communication skills).
- Wrote monthly newsletter on club activities and projects. Five thousand copies were distributed for each publication. Received the Best High Newspaper award (writing skills).
- Provided job performance feedback to each individual team member on a quarterly basis (leadership skills). The team was composed of **40** students.

Key roles include student council member, class president, committee leader/chairperson, club officer, team leader, community organizer, club treasurer/secretary, or any other position in which the student has the opportunity to lead a group of people to accomplish a given mission.

Since you have been following the High School Checklist, you should have already started to get involved in extracurricular activities. However, in Step 7 you are going to start tailoring those activities to the tasks listed in your career worksheet. This means that you are going to intentionally seek the extracurricular activities that will provide the setting for you to perform these tasks in order show future employers that you have done the job already, even though you just graduated. Once you select the appropriate extracurricular activity (e.g., internship, part-time, or volunteer work), you are going record all your experiences in the two forms provided: the Task Log and the Task Journal.

TASK LOG

Employers want to know where, when, and how well you have <u>performed</u> the tasks of the job they need to fill. The information recorded in this log will be transferred later to a resume or to a post-secondary school application. Complete a task log for <u>every extracurricular</u> activity you perform. Always write your <u>target tasks first</u> so you know what activities to aim for. Check out the following examples and instructions.

Target Tasks: (Example for Accounting)
• Complete income tax returns for individual clients and small businesses. • Audit clients' financial records for IRS compliance. • Create and analyze budgets. • Recommend methods to save money.

Note: Target tasks are taken from your Career Worksheet. They are to be used as a reference when selecting an extracurricular activity. The objective is to seek the setting that will give the opportunity to perform the targeted tasks. Write your target tasks at the header of your task log, as in the template provided.

Job Title	Income Tax Preparer
Date	January 2015 to present
Place	VITA* program, South Miami Branch. Volunteer Income Tax Assistance (VITA) provides free tax return preparation for people who need tax help but can't afford it. People with low to moderate incomes, seniors, people with disabilities, and those with limited English skills usually qualify for this free service. Volunteers receive specialized training directly from the IRS.
Tasks Completed	• Completed income tax returns for senior citizens and low-income families. Averaged **5** appointments per day. • Reviewed tax returns completed by other volunteer tax preparers to ensure that the tax returns were error-free. Averaged **20** audits per day.
Accomplishments	• Received **20** written compliments from clients, when the office average was **3**. • Was awarded with the **volunteer of the year award.** • Received **3** letters of commendation over a period of a month, one from each supervisor. • Was offered a full-time job position after college graduation. • Was selected in a group of **50** volunteers to receive the Tax Law Certification course given by the IRS headquarters in Washington, DC. • Promoted to tax auditor in just one month.

Job Title	Miami Warriors Club Treasurer
Date	October 2012 to March 2013
Place	Miami Senior High School
Tasks Completed	• Created and analyzed budgets. • Recommend methods to save money.
Accomplishments	• Cut the club expenses by **30%** • Implemented fundraising activities that brought an additional **$5,000** in donations from local businesses.

Job Title: Write the job titles you had during all of your extracurricular actitivies, including internships, volunteer work, and part-time work. Examples: Beta Club treasurer, school paper editor, teacher assistant, VITA tax preparer, sales associate, etc.

Date: Write down the timeframes for these positions.

Place: Write down the name of the place where you performed the work (paid and/or non-paid).

For organizations that are not easily recognized, write a brief description of what they do.

Example: VITA, nonprofit organization created by the IRS to assist seniors and low-income citizens with the filing of their taxes.

Also, if it is a large organization, identify the department you worked for.

For example: if you had a part-time job in Best Buy, you may want to specify which department you worked for (e.g., customer service department, home appliances, etc.).

Completed Tasks: Write the tasks you performed in each of these positions.

Use an action verb to document a task. Examples: Action verbs examples: Abbreviated, Abolished, Accepted, Accommodated, Accomplished, Acted, Activated, Adapted, Adhered, Adjusted, Administered, Advertised, Advised, Analyzed, Arranged, Assembled, Assisted, Built, Calculated, Captivated, Catalogued, Chaired, Coached, Compiled, Completed, Conceptualized, Conciliated, Conducted, Consulted, Contracted, Constructed, Created, Coordinated, Changed, Defined, Delegated, Demonstrated, Designed, Devised, Directed, Distributed, Drafted, Edited, Educated, Enlarged, Established, Evaluated, Executed, Examined, Expanded, Expedited, Explained, Facilitated, Formulated, Generated, Governed, Guided, Hired, Identified, Illustrated, Implemented, Improved, Increased, Indexed, Informed, Initiated, Innovated, Inspected, Installed, Integrated, Intensified, Interviewed, Investigated, Invented, Maintained, Managed, Marketed, Masterminded, Maximized, Mentored, Modified, Monitored, Motivated, Negotiated, Obtained, Orchestrated, Optimized, Organized, Pioneered, Prepared, Presented, Presided, Processed, Programmed, Proliferated, Promoted, Proposed, Publicized, Recaptured, Recommended, Recorded, Recruited, Rejuvenated, Related, Re-engineered, Revised, Specified, Stimulated, Structured, Surveyed, Supervised, Synthesized, Taught, Transmitted, Used, Wrote.

Also use numbers to <u>quantify your performance</u> at each task performed (e.g., trained **15** students, processed over **100** shipments, or answered **500** calls per day). Numbers get recognized and paid attention to at the time of transferring the information from your task log to your resume. This is why you write them in bold letters.

Accomplishments: Accomplishments are actions that improved or impacted the places you worked in terms of <u>productivity and efficiency</u> (time or money you saved), and/or any difficult problems you solved. Therefore, think of instances where you saved or earned extra money.

- Recommended new accounting software that reduced booking time from **3 hours to 1 hour.**

Think of instances where you solved a specific problem and how you did it.

- Transferred hard copy files to the school's cloud, addressing storage space problems and ease-of-access issues simultaneously.

Accomplishments are also any **special recognition you receive** (e.g., promotions, awards, commendations).

TASK LOG TEMPLATE

Target Tasks:
1. _____
2. _____
3. _____
4. _____

Job Title	
Date	
Place	
Tasks Completed	
Accomplishments	

TASK JOURNAL

The purpose of a task journal is to record what happened while you were performing the tasks documented in your Task Log. There might be a lapse of time between the time you performed the task and the time you are asked to talk about it, so to make sure you have something to say you need to record your experiences. Here is an example of what kind of experiences should be recorded and how they should be written.

Date: 9/16/15

Place: Best Buy, Home Appliances Department. (Provide the setting)

Position Title: Sales Associate (Define your role in the situation)

Situation	Upset customer because of a damaged 60" TV. The customer told me in a loud tone of voice: "I want my money back right now...I am taking my money someplace else!"
Actions	• Used active listening to validate the customer's concern. • Apologized for the incident (even though it was not my fault) to show ownership of the situation. • Explained my solution to the problem and the action I was going to take execute it to put him at ease. • Thanked the customer for bringing the matter to my attention.
Results	• Customer bought two others 60" TVs (over **$10,000.00** in sales in **1 day**). • Received **Salesman of the quarter award**

Situation: A challenge you encountered while performing one of the tasks in your log (e.g., a situation where you applied technical expertise to solve a problem). When recording a situation, consider the following:

- Stick to the facts and avoid personal opinions. For example, instead of saying that the customer was rude, say what really happened: customer told me in a loud tone of voice: "I want my money back right now...I am taking my money someplace else!" Keep in mind that what may seem rude to you might not necessarily be rude to other people.

- Use numbers to describe who and what was involved in the situation (e.g., impact to the place where you were working, or number of people affected). Example: a customer who just spent **$ 3,000.00** on a 60" TV was returning it and taking his business away to a competitive store. The company was losing **$3,000** in sales and a good client.

Actions

Your future employers want to see that your actions were not by chance, but by careful and effective thought process. They want to make sense of WHY you did what you did. Give yourself an opportunity to demonstrate your critical thinking skills (use of logic and reasoning to analyze the strengths and weaknesses of alternative solutions to a problem). Therefore, articulate the rationale behind your action using a sequential thought process, and do not use the plural, such as "we thought that..." or "our team decided that..." Instead, focus on your specific contributions to the solving of the problem.

Example:

- Actively listened to make the client feel validated.
- Apologized for the incident even though it was not my fault, showing ownership of the situation and taking responsibility.
- Explained what I was going to do for the client and how soon I was going to get it done to put the client at ease.
- Thanked the client for bringing the matter to my attention, to show accountability.
- Made a courtesy follow-up call the next day to make sure everything was going as planned and to make myself available if further assistance was needed.

Lastly, always emphasize the reason behind each action and how each of them progressively contributed to a successful outcome.

Results

➤ The outcome must be a direct result of your actions and not because of other factors (e.g., someone else's efforts or pure coincidence).

➤ Do not use the words *fewer* or *better*, instead use numbers, percentages, or any other statistics or data (e.g., "...because of my actions I was able to reduce the assembly time from **15 minutes** to **5 minutes**, or saved the company **$10 per unit** in production cost.").

➤ Provide concrete evidence of a succesful outcome (e.g., awarded employee of the month, received a letter of recommendation, was promoted to assistant supervisor, etc.).

➤ If the outcome was not positive, write what important lessons you learned from the experience. Make a note for yourself on how you are to respond next time if this situation was to present itself again.

➤ Emphasize how the results of your actions positively impacted the organization you were working for. Example: Customer decided to stay with the company and bought additional products resulting in **$5,000** in sales.

CAREER WORKSHEET EXAMPLES

Example# 1

Industry (Step 2)	Health Care Industry
Job Position (Step 5)	Registered Nurse
Post-Secondary School (Step 6)	University of Miami Nursing School
Target Tasks (Career Worksheet)	• Administer medications to patients and monitor for side effects. • Record medical information and vital signs. • Consult and coordinate with team members to assess, plan, implement, or evaluate patient care plans.
Extra-Curricular Activities (Steps 6-7)	Internship in the University of Miami Hospital (Required internship) Baptist Hospital Nurse Assistant (Volunteer work)

Note: Even though this occupation requires an internship as part of the curriculum, the student sought additional work experience through volunteer work.

Example # 2

Industry (Step 2)	Professional Services—Accounting
Job Position (Step 5)	Accountant
Post-Secondary School (Step 6)	• Miami-Dade Community College (Associate Degree) • Florida International University (Bachelor Degree)
Target Tasks (Career Worksheet)	• Complete income tax returns for individual clients and small businesses. • Audit clients' financial records for IRS compliance. • Create and analyze budgets. • Recommend methods to save money.
Extra-Curricular Activities (Step 7)	• Miami Warriors Club Treasurer (Senior year) • H&R Block Client Greeter (2016 Tax Season) • Part-time Bookkeeper for Johnson & Johnson Accounting firm • VITA Program Volunteer

Note: The training for this occupation does not include on-the-job experience; therefore, the student is responsible for seeking work experience independently. In this example, the student sought both paid and non-paid opportunities since high school (e.g., Miami Warriors Club and the VITA program. Refer to task log examples.).

CAREER WORKSHEET TEMPLATE

Industry (Step 2)	
Job Position (Step 5)	
Post-Secondary School (Step 6)	
Target Tasks (Career Worksheet)	
Extra-Curricular Activities (Step 7)	

CME GOAL

The CME goal should come as no surprise to you. When you are ready to apply for the job in your career worksheet, you are going to realize that you have already done most of the tasks listed in the job posting. Moreover, when you get called for the job interview, you are going to pull out that task journal that you have been filling out all along and will be able to talk about your experience on the job with great detail. The CME goal is achieved when your resume mirrors the actual job posting. A picture is worth a thousand words! Here is an example of what it is supposed to look like. Match list numbers between the job posting and the sample resume, seeing their relationship and verifying the fulfillment of the requirement. It is that simple!

Target Job	Your Resume
Job Positing: Certified Public Accountant	**Education**
Qualifications	1. Bachelor's Degree in Accounting, graduated in April 2013, University of Miami, Miami, Florida
1. Bachelor's Degree in Accounting	2. CPA* Certification, May 2015
2. CPA* Certified	
	Work Experience
Duties:	VITA* program January 2015 to present
1. Complete income tax returns for individual clients and small businesses.	Miami, Florida
	Income Tax Preparer
	1. Completed income tax returns for senior citizens and low-income families. Received **20** written compliments from clients, when the office average was **3**. Was awarded with the **volunteer of the year award**. **Promoted to tax auditor** in the **first month.**
2. Audit clients' financial records for IRS compliance.	2. Reviewed tax returns completed by other volunteer tax preparers to ensure that the tax returns were error-free. Averaged **20 audits per day**. Received **3 letters of commendation** from leadership over a period of **1 month** for finding and correcting discrepancies. Was selected from a group of **50** volunteers to received the **Tax Law Certification** course given by the **IRS** headquarters and to train other volunteers upon return. Was offered a full-time job position after graduation.
3. Create and analyze budgets.	
4. Recommend methods to save money and increase profit.	
	Miami Senior High School September 2012 to March 2013
	Miami Warriors Club Treasurer
	Largest club in the Miami community for high school students, with a membership of approximately **5,000 students** and a budget of **$100,000 a year.** The mission of the club is to feed the homeless and provide school supplies for children of low-income families.
	3. Created and analyzed the quarterly budget for the club.
	4. Recommended savings method that cut the club's expenses by **30%**. Implemented fundraising activities that brought an additional **$50,000** in donations.

THE HIGH SCHOOL TO-DO LIST

9th Grade To-Do-List

☐ N/A ☐	**Set up a study routine.** Note: Concentrate on good grades. Ninth grade goes on your official transcript (the history of the classes you have taken and the grades you have achieved). Post-secondary schools look at your transcript to determine whether you will be accepted into their programs and for scholarship purposes. They look at the quantity, diversity, and difficulty level of your classes. For those targeting an Ivy League school the process begins now, if not sooner.
☐ N/A ☐	**Get involved in activities outside the classroom/school.** Begin working toward leadership/key positions in the activities or organizations you identify yourself with. Become involved in your community.
☐ N/A ☐	**Complete Industry Research Activity found in Step 1.**
☐ N/A ☐	**Complete the Industry of Interest Activity in Step 2.** Document your industry of interest in your Career Worksheet.
☐ N/A ☐	Actively **participate in the class** and look for ways to contribute to it. If talking to your teacher doesn't come easy for you, make an effort (e.g., linger after class to discuss the day's lesson, etc.). This attitude produces letters of recommendation, favorable references, and even has an effect on your grades. Teachers' letters of recommendation/awards are later added to your resume and college admission package.
☐ N/A ☐	Start a filing system to save your best work/accomplishments (e.g., awards, recognitions, etc.). This includes documentation of any activity that relates, supports, or could be relevant to an employer or a competitive secondary school for admission purposes.

10th Grade To-Do List

☐ N/A ☐	Discuss with your parents and guidance counselor your goals for the year. **Incorporate your industry research findings into your class selections as electives.** Examples may include a Microsoft Office class, keyboarding, foreign language, etc. Notify your high school counselor of your industry of interest for class recommendations within the Department of Education Career cluster. This also includes a review of course requirements. May need to take geometry (if not already done so), biology, and the second year of a foreign language.
☐ N/A ☐	**Establish your study routine.**
☐ N/A ☐	**Decide on a weekly review date to go through previous week's tasks and plan for the coming one.**
☐ N/A ☐	**Enroll in extracurricular activities.** Continue working toward leadership/key positions within organizations/activities you chose in 9th grade. Become more involved in your community.
☐ N/A ☐	**Continue in your efforts to become more involved in the classroom**, increasing class participation and contribution.
☐ N/A ☐	**Complete the Employer List Activity in Step 3.**
☐ N/A ☐	**Complete Job List activity in Step 4.**
☐ N/A ☐	**Complete the Educational Path activity in Step 5.**
☐ N/A ☐	**Complete the Step 5 Job Shadowing activity.**
☐ N/A ☐	**Complete the Tasks-skills match activity in Step 5.**
☐ N/A ☐	**Document job in your career worksheet.**
☐ N/A ☐	**Conduct Step 5 informational interviews.**
☐ N/A ☐	**If applicable, decide on a major.**
☐ N/A ☐	**Complete the CME school test, Step 6.**
☐ N/A ☐	If applicable, **take SAT Subject Test** (offered in May and June) for the courses completed during the year. SAT Subject Tests measure the student's knowledge of a specific academic subject; required for admission and/or placement. See admission requirements for the college of your choice.
☐ N/A ☐	**Save your best work/accomplishments** (e.g., awards, recognitions, etc.) to your files.
☐ N/A ☐	**Contact your selected college/technical school to ask for academic admission requirements.** Meet with a representative for specific admission recommendations.
☐ N/A ☐	**Plan for selected school admission required courses or prerequisites with your counselor.**
☐ N/A ☐	Plan for extracurricular activities for next year.

11th Grade To-Do List

Fall

☐ N/A ☐	**Meet with your school counselor to review pending courses and selected school admission required courses or prerequisites.** This is the best time to take advantage of AP classes (if applicable) and get the scores in time for the college application. There will be lots of distractions in your senior year.
☐ N/A ☐	**Stay involved in your extracurricular activities.** Post-secondary schools like to see consistency and progression in responsibilities within a selected organization. Also plan for extracurricular activities for your senior year.
☐ N/A ☐	Visit www.collegeboard.org. **Review tools, applications, and resources such as:** The Official SAT Question of the Day, My College Search, Quick Start™, and My Organizer. Download a practice test. Read the free booklet: *Getting Ready for the SAT*
☐ N/A ☐	(October) **Take the PSAT/NMSQT for the National Merit Scholarship Program and practice** The ACT is a college entrance examination. Consult the *Preparing for the ACT* free guide for test content, format description, administration procedures, and practice tests. Both the ACT and the SAT are used to <u>predict college success</u> and can be noted later in your resume as a career accomplishment (in the case of an exceptional score). The SAT assesses the student's readiness for college-level courses and supports the college admission decision. The Preliminary SAT/National Merit Scholarship Qualifying Test (NMSQT), known as the PSAT, is the practice test for the SAT.
☐ N/A ☐	If applicable, **prepare for the ACT exam by taking the American College Testing program's PLAN (Pre-ACT) assessment program.**
☐ N/A ☐	If applicable, **start the certification process for Division I or Division II of college sports.** Ensure that your core curriculum meets the National Collegiate Athletic Association (NCAA) requirements.
☐ N/A ☐	Begin learning with your parents about financial aid. **Develop a financial aid plan; include a list of the aid sources, requirements for each application, and a timetable for meeting filing deadlines.**

Winter

☐ N/A ☐	If applicable, **discuss your ACT/SAT scores with your high school counselor, your parents, and your selected college advisor to decide if you should try to improve your scores by taking them again during the winter or the spring.** Two scores before the summer will give a clear idea of where you stand. The next test may not be until October of your senior year.
☐ N/A ☐	If applicable, **register for the ACT** at www.actstudent.org (Offered in April or June). Take it again in the fall of your senior year, if necessary.
☐ N/A ☐	**Begin your scholarships search now to reduce student loans.** The more you apply, the more chances you have to win. Investigate every scholarship sponsor. NEVER provide your credit card or bank account number on the telephone to an organization you have not researched. If a request for money is made by phone, the organization is probably fraudulent. Be suspicious if the sponsor's address is a P.O. Box number or a residential address.

Sprint

☐ N/A ☐	If applicable, **begin drafting your college essay.** Consult with your guidance counselor, your English teacher, and your selected college representative for ideas and guidance. Consider the personal essay you wrote for your English class.
☐ N/A ☐	**Discuss your PSAT score with your parents and high school counselor** (if taken in October). Incorporate your findings (strengths and weaknesses) in your preparation strategy to take the actual SAT in early January. Consider how your score matches the scores of accepted students at a targeted post-secondary school.
☐ N/A ☐	**Register for the SAT if you plan to take it in March.**
☐ N/A ☐	**If English is not your primary language, plan to take the TOEFL test.** The **TOEFL** is used to test English as a Foreign Language. TOEFL's scores help interpret scores on the verbal sections of the SAT. Go to www.toefl.org for more information.
☐ N/A ☐	(February) **Decide on which teachers to ask for letters of recommendation.**
☐ N/A ☐	(February) **Register to take the Advanced Placement Exams** given in May.
☐ N/A ☐	(February) **Take the SAT Subject Tests now** in the spring while course information is still fresh.
☐ N/A ☐	Register for the SAT and/or SAT Subject Tests if planning to take them in May.
☐ N/A ☐	(April) Register for the SAT and/or SAT subject Tests if planning takes them in June.
☐ N/A ☐	(April) **Plan your courses for senior year according to selected post-secondary school requirements.**

☐ N/A ☐	(May) If applicable, **discuss with your coach and counselor NCAA requirements for college sports Division I or Division II.**
☐ N/A ☐	(May) Begin planning for a summer job or volunteer work.
☐ N/A ☐	If applicable, contact your counselor to talk about military academies or ROTC scholarships.

Summer

☐ N/A ☐	**Register for the SAT and/or SAT Subject if planning to take them in October or November**
☐ N/A ☐	If applicable, register with the NCAA Eligibility Center (www.ncaa.org) for NCAA Division I or II of college sport. (See information for athletes below).
☐ N/A ☐	Record in your year's accomplishments, activities, and work experiences. List activities that show the most consistent involvement and demonstrate your leadership abilities (refer to task log and task journal).

INFORMATION FOR ATHLETES

Learn the academic requirements and SAT/ACT scores for the NCAA certification and plan accordingly. Begin working on the following attributes:

- Team-building skills
- Academic excellence
- Optimal height and weight
- Attitude in games/matches and practice, attendance, discipline, etc.
- Attitude toward coaching staff

College athletic programs are regulated by the National Collegiate Athletic Association (NCAA). This is the organization that establishes the rules on eligibility, recruitment, and financial aid for the program. Student athletes must be certified by the NCAA Eligibility Center. Begin the process by sending a completed Student Release Form to the NCAA Eligibility Center. This form authorizes the release of transcripts, test scores, proof of grades, and any other academic information to both the NCAA and your selected school. ACT and/or SAT score reports must be sent directly to the NCAA from the testing center. Make sure to select classes that meet NCAA requirements. The center will make a certification decision and report directly to the institution. Review the *Guide for the College-Bound Student Athlete* at www.ncaa.org for details and updated information.

National Association of Intercollegiate Athletics (NAIA) Eligibility Requirements

Meet two of the following three requirements.

1. Minimum overall high school grade point average of 2.0 on a 4.0 scale.
2. Composite score of 18 or higher on the ACT or total score of 860 or higher on the SAT Critical Reading and Math sections.
3. Final class rank in the top half of the graduating class.

Students must have their test score sent to the school admission office directly from the testing center.

Getting Athletic Scholarship Recommendations

1. Contact the head coaches of the selected school.
2. Write an athletic resume highlighting your accomplishments.
3. Put together 10 to 15 minutes of video highlights of your athletic performance.
4. Get letters of recommendation from your coaches.
5. Conduct regular follow-ups during your senior year.

12th Grade To-Do-List

☐ N/A ☐	(September) **Begin an Activity Chart/Calendar** to track admission requirements, financial aid, and scholarships deadlines, etc., for your selected school(s). **Check deadlines and organize your application tasks in chronological order** (earliest due date first).
☐ N/A ☐	(September or October) **Review your transcript.** Get an unofficial copy of your transcript. Check personal information, titles of courses, community service hours, etc. Check that <u>no</u> courses taken have been left out, and check that your grades are accurate. The transcript should also include class ranking, grade point average, and an official record of your ACT and/or SAT scores (if applicable). Take any corrections or questions back to your counselor. Make all corrections by October 1.
☐ N/A ☐	**Ask for letters of recommendation** from your counselor, teachers, coaches, and/or employers (mid-September is a good time). ✓ Provide recommendation forms along with a stamped self-addressed envelope. ✓ Talk to the ones who are aware of your goals and/or for whom you worked the hardest, or have produced your best work. Mention application deadlines and do a follow-up (mark it in your calendar about a week before it is due). ✓ Provide a copy of your resume (stressing your best work, accomplishments, and contributions to the class for your teacher to use as a reference).
☐ N/A ☐	(October) If applicable, **register for the SAT and/or SAT Subject Tests** to take them again in December or January.
☐ N/A ☐	If applicable, write the **first draft of your college essay** and ask your parents, English teacher, and counselor to review it.
☐ N/A ☐	If applicable, **fill out the CSS/Financial Aid PROFILE**, at www.collegeboard.org (starting Oct. 1). The PROFILE (usually required by highly selective schools) goes into detail about home equity, retirement accounts, noncustodial parents, and other information not included in the federal financial aid application. Since the information is used for institutional grants and scholarships controlled by the school, contact selected colleges to be sure you have filed the required forms.

☐ N/A ☐	**Complete the Free Application for Federal Student Aid (FAFSA)** at www.fafsa.ed.gov. You will reapply every year. Collect and organize your personal information before sitting down to fill out the application. Double check entries to make sure the information is correct.
☐ N/A ☐	(November) If applicable, **finish your application essay.**
☐ N/A ☐	(November) If applicable, **ensure that test scores will be sent by the testing agency to the designated school(s).** For the SAT and the ACT, send your highest score. Document latest college board test dates and scores. Write down your high school's College Examination Board (CEB) number (usually stamped on the front of your SAT and ACT packets).
☐ N/A ☐	(November) **Provide your counselor the proper forms to send transcripts to your selected college(s) to meet deadlines** (at least two weeks in advance, if no deadline is in place by the guidance office). Verify that all forms are in order and set up a follow-up date to ensure they were sent on time. Include letters of recommendation, an essay, the secondary school report form, and midyear school report (sent by your guidance counselor after you fill out a portion of the form).
☐ N/A ☐	(December) **Get the FAFSA PINs** for you and your parents at www.pin.ed.gov
☐ N/A ☐	(December) If early decision application was denied (usually by Dec. 15), this is the time to **submit applications to other schools.**
☐ N/A ☐	**Apply for the scholarships to meet application deadlines.** For example: ROTC scholarships offer up to a four-year scholarship that pays full college tuition plus a monthly allowance. These scholarships are based on GPA, class rank, ACT or SAT scores, and physical qualifications. Apply before December 1.
☐ N/A ☐	(December) **Gather information to file taxes early and complete your FAFSA:** W-2; 1099s; untaxed income; bank accounts; debts; and investments. Consider filing based on income estimates, if parents are self-employed or can't get taxes done before the deadline. Keep in mind that if your estimate is significantly off, eligibility may have to be recalculated, delaying the process.
☐ N/A ☐	(December) **Contact the financial aid office at your selected school(s) to see if they require any other financial aid forms.**
☐ N/A ☐	(January) **Submit your FAFSA** if the school has a financial aid deadline of Feb. 1.

□ N/A □	(January) If applicable, **submit any other required financial aid forms** such as PROFILE or the school's own forms. Keep copies.
□ N/A □	(January) If selected school(s) requires midyear grades, give the form to your school counselor. **Maintain or improve your GPA**; schools reserve the right to cancel offers to students who fall below the standard during the second semester (may receive a letter of probation; for most competitive schools, admissions are contingent on final grades). Do not drop challenging classes (a drastic change in your schedule may require an explanation).
□ N/A □	(February) If applicable, **let your selected school know of any honors courses/ accomplishments not included in the submitted application.**
□ N/A □	(February) **Contact school to verify that all application materials** have been received.
□ N/A □	(February) **Correct or update your Student Aid Report** (SAR).
□ N/A □	(February) **Inform your selected school financial office of any special circumstance** (e.g., a future medical procedure that may incur large expenses. Some schools may adjust the financial aid formula if the situation is valid and well documented).
□ N/A □	(February) **File income tax returns.** Some schools may require copies of your family's returns before finalizing financial aid offers.
□ N/A □	If applicable, **register for AP exams.** (If you are homeschooled or your school does not offer AP, contact AP Services by March 1.
□ N/A □	Applicable to males only, **register for the selective service** on your eighteenth birthday (required for federal and state financial aid).

□ N/A □	**Monitor your financial aid application.** Make sure to receive your FAFSA acknowledgement. Review all correspondence; some may require action on your part.
□ N/A □	**Monitor your application status** (updates may be available online at the school website). **Review all correspondence**; some may require action on your part.
□ N/A □	(March) If required, **send copies of your FAFSA to the scholarships for which you have applied.**
□ N/A □	(March) Send midyear grade report to selected school(s).
□ N/A □	(May) If applicable, **send your AP Grade Report to your selected school(s).** AP Exams are given in May.
□ N/A □	(June) Have your counselor **send your final transcript to your selected school(s).**
□ N/A □	(June) If applying for Division I or Division II college sports, **send your final transcript to the NCAA Eligibility Center.**
□ N/A □	If applicable, **consider taking the College-Level Examination Program (CLEP). This test** allows students to earn college credit for what they already know (whether it was learned in school, through independent study, or through experiences outside the classroom). For information visit http://clep.collegeboard.org

TEACHER RECOMMENDATIONS

Make a personal request to your teachers and provide them a copy of your resume, class accomplishment records/contribution log or best work, as applicable. Use your task log and task journal as a reference. Some counselors/teachers provide students an essay question to give them the background they need for a recommendation. Find out which approach is used at your school. Follow targeted school's instructions regarding the exact number and consider the following recommendations:

- Select the teachers that know you best.
- Select teachers that have taught you for more than one course and have watched your skills develop.
- Select teachers that have sponsored the extracurricular activities you have participated in.
- Select the subject-area teachers required by your targeted school.
- Select the subject-area teachers related to your major (if applicable).
- Get recommendations from your employer, your rabbi or pastor, or volunteer work supervisor.

LETTER OF RECOMMENDATION TRACKING SHEET TEMPLATE

Letters of recommendations	Name (teacher/counselor/supervisor)	Date requested	Followed-up Date
Letters of recommendation 1			
Letters of recommendation 2			

TRACKING SHEETS TEMPLATE

Make yourself various checklists to capture the items you need to keep track of. Adapt the following examples to your unique situation. Here are two examples:

School Enrollment Checklist	Completion date
Test scores requested	
Official transcript sent	
Letters of recommendation sent	
Essay completed and sent	
SAT/ACT scores sent	
All signatures collected	
Copies made of all forms and documentation enclosed in application packet	
Application fee enclosed	
Tuition deposit sent	
Application packet submitted	
Letters of acceptance received	
(if applicable) Housing and other forms submitted to chosen school	
Orientation scheduled	

FINANCIAL AID AND SCHOLARSHIP APPLICATIONS CHECKLIST TEMPLATES

Items to Track	Deadline	Date Received	Date completed/Sent
Free Application for Federal Student Aid (FAFSA) and/or PROFILE® Forms			
Changes made, if needed			
Financial Award Letters			

Essays
(For admission and/or scholarship purposes)

- Pick a topic you truly care about.
- Don't be too critical, pessimistic, or antagonistic. Example: If addressing a social issue, offer solutions; if the story doesn't have a happy ending, focus on what you learned from the experience and how you would do things differently if faced with a similar situation in the future; and if you had a difficult childhood, talk about how you overcame those challenges and how you want to help others deal with the same hardships (talk about how the experience made you wiser, stronger, and/or more compassionate toward others).
- Your "living with purpose" attitude, commitment, and perseverance are the character traits that make the scholarship-awarding committee give you the money. Both scholarships and admission are granted to students who understand what they are doing and why they are doing it; someone who is committed to a given life goal, has a defined purpose in life, and has demonstrated having the inner strength to persevere to the end. This is what sets apart one candidate from another.
- Focus on a specific and concrete aspect of your life (e.g., a unique quality, but not a list of all your accomplishments). Talk about things you did that demonstrate leadership and initiative and the impact they had. An extracurricular activity, such as volunteer work or working part-time to help support your family illustrates your priorities and lets the scholarship selection committee know what's important to you.
- Proofread several times. Put the essay aside for a few days then come back to it.
- Follow instructions (specified topic and length) and make sure your essay connects your personal skills, characteristics, and experiences with the scholarship's objectives (the reason the scholarship exits). Do research on the organization sponsoring it.

Essay Sample Topics	Recommendations
Tell us about yourself.	Describe your personality, background, accomplishments, and goals. Talk about how a certain character/personality trait is going to be a decisive factor in achieving your goals. Write also about an experience that helped shape your character and goals, or about something you have learned from your parents that influenced you the most.
Tell us about an academic or extracurricular interest.	Explain how a book, an experience, or an ideology shaped your vision and purpose in life. For example, a student may discuss how having a sibling with a learning disability motivated him or her to use technology as a means to diversify teaching methods, or may use an experience in sports to tell how he or she learned the value of teamwork.
Tell us why you want to come to our college.	Explain how your goals and interests match the objectives of the school/scholarship. Outline the aspects of your background (accomplishments, academic performance, and work experience) and how they will contribute to the program (what you have to offer).

FINANCIAL AID

The financial aid advisor is the professional in the best position to answer questions about the financial aid application process, review applications for mistakes, educate you about the different financing packages available, and make recommendations based on their experience, training, and your specific financial situation. If you are a qualified candidate with the potential to make the school look good, they will make every effort possible to ensure that you get the money you need to pay tuition. Secondary education institutions, whether they are universities or vocational schools, do compete against each other for business. Their prestige and ranking in the market is determined, for the most part, by the quality of the students they attract (e.g., class ranking, SAT scores, GPA, etc.). So, as a business marketing strategy, schools create incentives for those students with the best overall profiles within the constraints of the school's revenue goals. Review the following basic financial aid definitions before meeting with your school financial aid advisor.

Federal Scholarships: Scholarships are awarded for academic excellence or any other special talents or abilities. Repayment is not required.

Federal Grants: Federal government financial assistance granted to students with financial need. Grants do not have to be repaid. The Federal Pell Grant is the most common grant program. Eligibility depends on the expected family contribution (EFC) and other factors, such as tuition cost, and full-time/part-time status. However, the actual awarded amounts ultimately depend on how much funding is allocated by Congress each year.

Loans: Student loans are issued through commercial lending institutions and the Department of Education. Students begin repaying the loan after graduation or when they leave the school without finishing. There are two types of loans; subsidized and unsubsidized. Subsidized loans are for those who have special financial needs, and unsubsidized loans are available to everyone. Loan interest on a subsidized loan does not begin to accrue until the student is no longer in school, while the interest on an unsubsidized loan begins to accrue upon disbursement of funds.

HIGH SCHOOL TO-DO LIST FOR PARENTS

☐ N/A ☐	**Have a discussion to set goals for the year.** Write down a list of the things your son or daughter wants to accomplish (e.g., take some honors classes, become an editor for the school newspaper, etc.). Goals give your child something to work toward and stay motivated.
☐ N/A ☐	**Decide on a weekly review date to go through the previous week's tasks and plan for the coming one.**
☐ N/A ☐	**Assist your child in setting up a system to organize assignments, test dates, and extracurricular activities.** Make recommendations as to what he or she needs to do and how much time he or she has to do it. Teach your child about prioritizing and time management skills. This also includes providing the supplies and technology to get the schoolwork done.
☐ N/A ☐	**Establish with your child a study routine.** Exercise discipline (example, playing video games after chores and homework) and foster consistent study habits. Nobody in college or any secondary school is going to hound your child down to complete an assignment; this is the time to set a good foundation and develop the study patterns that lead to success, if it hasn't been done already.
☐ N/A ☐	**Teach your child self-advocacy skills** so that he or she learns how to deal with some issues alone. Example: If you need something, you need to speak up and talk to your teacher/school administrator. If you are struggling in a particular subject, you need to ask your teacher for extra help. There are resources available to you. Your school counselor is equipped to help you figure out any situation you may encounter in school (e.g., bullies, interpersonal issues, etc.).
☐ N/A ☐	**Seek expert advice** (School guidance counselor) and follow their recommendation as any of the following situations with your child arises. • Your child is experiencing disciplinary issues. • Your child is not performing well academically or he or she is having learning issues. Recommendations can range from special classes to improve your child's skills in specific areas, to various types of assessments, counseling, and academic tutoring, to specific strategies to deal with your child's behavior. (See **Students with Special Needs**).

□ N/A □	**Encourage and support extracurricular activities.** Post-secondary schools look for not only academically talented students, but also those who are well-rounded. That is, students who are involved and active in their communities. They consider the person as a whole. Advice your child to start with a few activities, then gradually increase involvement as he or she moves toward graduation. The goal is to achieve a leadership/key position (e.g., president, treasurer, etc.) by senior year. These key positions are not only considered as concrete evidence of success, but also provide a valid context where employable skills can be accounted for. Extracurricular activities count for actual work experience, depending on the job function.
□ N/A □	**Learn about Honors and College Advanced Placement (AP) courses.** Competitive post-secondary schools not only look at the final GPA, but also at how your child challenged himself or herself. Did your child take courses that stretched them academically, such as honors and AP classes, or did they just take the easy route of the minimum requirements? There are regular classes (standard requirement for graduation) and honors classes (in-depth knowledge of a particular academic subject by means of research and investigation). Be aware of the academic <u>expectations</u> for honors classes and consider whether your child has what it takes to succeed. **Request the assistance of your child's counselor for class selection and to set <u>realistic goals.</u>** The Advanced Placement (AP) courses allow high school students to earn college credits while in high school. AP courses are offered in the following subject areas: Art History, Biology, Calculus AB, Calculus BC, Chemistry, Chinese Language and Culture, Computer Science, English Language and Composition, English Literature and Composition, Environmental Science, European History, French Language, German Language, Government and politics: Comparative, Government and Politics: United States, Human Geography, Italian Language and Culture, Japanese Language and Culture, Latin Vergil, Macroeconomics, Microeconomics, Music Theory, Physics B, Physics C: Electricity and Magnetism, Physics C: Mechanics, Psychology, Spanish Language, Spanish Literature, Statistics, Studio Art: 2-Design, Studio Art: 3-D Design, Studio Art: Drawing, United States History, and World History. Find out which AP courses are available in your school. If you achieve a qualifying score in the AP exam, you may be able to waive some introductory college courses, saving you <u>time and money</u>. AP courses are considered **<u>evidence of success/accomplishments</u>** for both prospective employers and prestigious post-secondary schools. **Plan/prepare for AP classes (junior and senior years) by enrolling and doing well in honors classes during your 9th and 10th grades.**

☐ N/A ☐	**Support every career exploration opportunity.** Conduct career research with your son or daughter. Become your child's industry research partner. Activities may include: • Shadow someone in the workplace. • Check out and monitor the construction of a building project and if possible, talk to the people involved. • Check out professional conventions. • Tour a manufacturing facility. • Surf the Internet. • Subscribe to a professional association magazine. • View educational TV programs, reality TV shows such as *24/7* and *Undercover Boss*. • Go to open houses sponsored by local businesses. • Visit a medical facility. • Attend open houses of new plants or additions to facilities. • Conduct an information interview with individuals on their jobs.

STUDENTS WITH SPECIAL NEEDS

By definition, a student is considered to have a disability if he or she has a documented physical or mental impairment that substantially limits one or more major life activities: personal self-care, walking, seeing, hearing, speaking, breathing, learning, working, or performing manual tasks; or he or she is perceived as having such impairments. Other less obvious disabilities include diabetes, asthma, multiple sclerosis, heart disease, cancer, mental illness, mental retardation, cerebral palsy, and learning disabilities. A learning disability is a condition that impedes a person's ability to process and disseminate information. It is recognized as a significant deficiency in one or more of the following areas: oral expression, listening comprehension, written expression, basic reading skills, reading comprehension, mathematical calculation, and problem solving. Students with a learning disability may also have difficulty with sustained attention, time management/organization, and/or social skills.

Following a series of assessments, an individualized educational plan (IEP) for your son or daughter's unique situation will be implemented by the school administration. The value of an IEP resides in that the delivery of certain services is coordinated in a way that your teen gets to work with professionals with different areas of expertise (e.g., speech pathologist and special education teachers with the training to teach your child the strategies he or she needs to succeed academically or in any other areas he or she is struggling). An (IEP) usually includes:

- Yearly educational goals based on your child's specific situation.
- Services involved in helping you achieve these goals, and what professionals are going to be delivering these services.
- Descriptions of specific strategies and accommodations to be implemented in the class, to include teaching recommendations for the teachers.
- Vocational assessment results and recommendations.
- Career training and/or on-the-job training coordination.

Students with disabilities have the right to receive accommodations and services that enable them to benefit from all programs offered, if academically qualified.

For parents: If your son or daughter has a disability, you will take the same CME steps to choose a secondary education school as other students; the only difference is that you will also evaluate your options based on how the school(s) meets your son or daughter's specific educational needs.

BEST PRACTICES FOR STUDENTS WITH SPECIAL NEEDS

- Document every disability with letters from a service provider (e.g., physicians, therapist, case manager, etc.). Describe the student's disability in a letter attached to the application so the admissions department can determine if there is a proper fit between the student's profile and the school's available programs. A psycho-educational evaluation and testing record may be required.

- Learn all federal laws that apply to students with disabilities.

- Locate a support group for local students with disabilities for information and advocacy. Talk to current students who have similar disabilities to hear about their experiences with the school under consideration.

- Contact the school's student with disabilities service office to discuss specific requirements. Then, evaluate how the school's policies, procedures, and facilities meet those specific needs. Accommodations may include flexible/individualized study plans, remedial courses, reduced course loads, and additional access to professors.

- Obtain letters of support from teachers, family, friends, and physicians to provide evidence of the student's academic success despite the disability.

ONLINE RESOURCES FOR STUDENTS WITH SPECIAL NEEDS

Organization	Website	Overview
Association on higher education and disability	www.ahead.org	Delivers training to higher education institutions through workshops, publications, and consultation.
Children and adults with attention-deficit/ hyperactivity disorder (CHADD)	www.chadd.org	Provides information, resources and networking opportunities to help families cope with Attention Deficit Hyperactivity Disorder. These resources include: • A *Call Center* with specialists who respond to questions. • An *Ask the expert webcast series* featuring leading ADHD scientists and researchers. • *YouTube videos* with ADHD information for educators. • *Fact Sheets* on specialized ADHD topics.
Heath resource center online clearinghouse on post-secondary education for individual with disabilities	www.heath.gwu.edu	Provides training sessions, and workshops; develops training modules; publishes resource papers, fact sheets, directories, and website information; Their focus is on accessibility, career development, classroom and laboratory accommodations, financial aid, independent living, transition resources, training and post-secondary education, career/technical education, and rehabilitation services.
Learning disabilities association of America (LDA)	www.ldanatl.org	LDA is committed to protecting the rights of students with learning disabilities. They promote ongoing research and disseminate their findings. Services include parent support, an informational and referral network, and school program development.
National center for learning disabilities (NCLD)	www.ncld.org	NCLD provides public awareness and grants to support research and innovative practices for students with disabilities.
National Organization for Disability (NOD)	www.nod.org	Known for its standard-setting data and its in-class disability employment models. Their focus is on increasing employment for individuals with disabilities who are not employed.
The international dyslexia association (IDA)	www.interdys.org	Promotes teaching approaches and clinical educational strategies for dyslexics based on research.

FINAL MESSAGE FOR STUDENTS

Did you graduate from the school you selected in Step 6? Congratulations! The time to apply to the job you have been targeting all along has finally come (Step 4). A good place to start is the employer list you created in Step 3. And of course, don't leave out the people you listed in your networking contact list (Step 2). They need to know that you graduated and are looking for a job.

CME is not the end of the career decision process, but the beginning. Once your career is set on a particular industry, there will be plenty of movement opportunities to look forward to as you position yourself where you want to be (e.g., specializing in a certain area or occupation within an industry, as in Step 2). One last thing; don't forget your task log and journal (Step 7). Now is the time to put them to work, writing your resume and preparing for your first job interview.

Good luck!

FINAL MESSAGE FOR PARENTS

Parents, CME wants to thank you for stepping up to the plate. The following is just a summary of what you just accomplished.

- Assisted your child in choosing an industry in demand in which to launch his or her career.
- Provided the experience that confirmed their unique abilities and interest, and guided him or her to choose an occupation were those unique abilities can be utilized to their full potential.
- Supervised the interactions with the different collaboration partners to ensure that their recommendations were in your child's best interest (e.g., school counselors, career coaches, etc.).
- Helped your child choose the best possible school to be trained in.
- Set the "working hard" attitude from the beginning and enforced the study habits that will be determinant in your child's success.
- Helped your child identify the obstacles that were hindering their career progress, depression, anxiety, self-esteem issues and guided him or her to seek the appropriate help.

One thing is left for you to do. Enjoy the benefits of a job well done.

Congratulations!!!!

ENDNOTES

1   Source: **Agglomeration and Job Matching among College Graduates.** Jaison R. Abel and Richard Deitz. *Federal Reserve Bank of New York Staff Reports*, no. 587 December 2012; revised December 2014. JEL classification: I21, J24, J31, R23

2   Source: Nick Anderson September 24, 2014. Washington Post. *National student loan default rate dips to 13.7 percent; still "too high" official says.*

CPSIA information can be obtained
at www.ICGtesting.com
Printed in the USA
BVHW012324130219
540211BV00007B/33/P

9 781645 165040